KV-374-919

CONTENTS

PART 2: *Making better work-life decisions*

Happy at Work?

Work-Life Balance, Time-Off, Retirement,
Money & Leisure

Andy Gibb

Cover photo: *Intrepid* pursuing the ship *Great Happy*

Published by Andy Gibb
Publishing partner: Paragon Publishing, Rothersthorpe
First published 2016
© Andy Gibb 2016

ISBN 978-1-78222-491-4

Book design, layout and production management by Into Print
www.intoprint.net
+44 (0)1604 832149

Printed and bound in UK and USA by Lightning Source

Books by Andy Gibb
www.intrepidofdover.co.uk

Get That Job
Intrepid Sailing around the World

Are you Happy at Work?

IF YOU ARE only working to achieve your goal, what is your goal?
Have you ever wondered what you are working for? Or what you want to achieve in life? These are fundamental questions. The American Constitution suggests the Pursuit of Happiness. This book explores some of these questions and some of the answers. I am a psychologist, director, and a sailor, so I searched into the psychology of why we set ourselves targets, when stress can be good and bad, and what makes us happy, and tested this by sailing around the world. I also examined the question of money – how much money do we need to achieve our dream, and how do we know when and if we can shift focus from work to leisure.

In many novels the main character dreams of buying a sail boat and sailing away. In real life, we may feel trapped and dream of getting away from it all. Getting away or stopping work is a powerful idea. But would it make us any happier? Is it realistic? And if it is realistic, why don't more people do it, if so many dream about it? Stopping work is often something that is done to us by redundancy or retirement age, rather than by our own conscious choice, how can we control our life to get a decent Work Life Balance?

We may dream of gardening or cultivating land or living the self-sufficient good life. Creating the perfect first or second home and having friends, children or grandchildren come to visit are other dreams. Starting our own company, getting involved in a charity, getting our golf handicap down, or our body into shape, or learning a language or a musical instrument, climbing Mount Everest while we are still young enough to do it, the list is endless. Before we get carried away, getting out of debt, or stress or depression, or into good health may be the top priority for many.

But sailing or travel still figures in many people's ambitions. As a work psychologist with 2 major international organizations, I listened to many ambitions and dreams, some realized, some put on the back burner, some quietly dropped. And I had my own ambition – to sail around the world.

In the end I sailed 50,000 miles around the world meeting fascinating people, both those sailing and those in the countries we visited. I listened to how they made it work, or in some cases how it hadn't worked. And I researched the psychology and conducted a survey to see how it fitted with the lives of the people I met, and how they had decided to live their life. I returned to work in a major hedge fund just as the financial crisis exploded, to check out the return to work in practice, and later, revised some figures to allow for inflation and exchange rates etc.

The result is this book. It is input to a strategy for work and life. It describes many of the factors that we need to be aware of if we are embarking on a new career, are considering a major change, or have it thrust upon us, perhaps by downsizing or stopping work; or a new partner or moving house or anything else. We normally identify targets and achievements that will we think make us happy or satisfied, so this is the fundamental aim in most cases, although we may not recognize this. Achieving sales or profit growth or promotion or a new start up or app is normally a means to an end, not an end in itself.

There are three Parts. Part 1 looks at what influences our happiness, and crucially which has most effect. It includes Work, Money, Control, Personality and Values, Friends and Family, Marriage, Children, Health, Religion and Exercise. Part 2 looks at work-life balance decisions, and how our mind works to protect ourselves; why our memory is seldom an accurate record, so that we remember things differently to how they occurred, explain events in ways that are counter-productive, and make decisions based on advertising or status concerns - factors that rationally have little bearing on what we are trying to do. Part 3 then asks 'How can we apply this practically so that we get more out of work and life, and when and how to get a better Work Life Balance?

I am not advocating stopping work, or being so self-centred that we ignore others. If we find our work fully satisfying, then we should continue. But it does suggest that if our work is not giving us enough satisfaction, we would be sensible to look at alternatives, which may include moving to a new job, taking a sabbatical, taking a longer period of time off, working part time or stopping full time work altogether.

This is not just theory, I have tested this in real life, and explored with many others their experiences of living the dream - the practicalities, like how much money it takes, how much time, what are the problems. Also the highs – the times you wouldn't trade for anything, the times that make it all worthwhile. And the scary times, frustrating times, and times when it all seems to be going wrong.

So if you or your partner are stressed at work, stuck in a dreary office, away from your friends and family more than you would like, seeing motorways, airports, hotels factories and offices more than beaches, ski-slopes, coral reefs and green fields; focused to the maximum extent on targets, costs, deadlines, and critical meetings, and feeling that some-how your work life balance isn't giving you the happiness that deep down you know it should, this book will give you a few ideas and enable you to put details onto your ambition for work and life whatever it is.

And if work has suddenly stopped, or will soon finish for whatever reason, (and increasingly this is outside our control) this book shows how to apply many of the same approaches that work in business to achieving what is most important – the life you want to lead for yourself and those you care about.

Andy Gibb

Part One:

What makes us Happy?

Intrepid of Dover beating to windward British Virgin Islands
2016

1. The Principles behind the Dream

> 'It was one of the best experiences of my life. When we arrived at the first of the 6 massive locks in the Panama Canal, it was totally dark, big ships were steaming past both ways in the narrow 80-metre-wide entrance channel, rain was teeming down making it difficult to see clearly, the wind was 30 knots gusting 40, and there was a two-hour unexplained delay during which we had to avoid being run down by large ships themselves battling the wind. Tugboats and crew boats jostled us and each other in this channel just a few metres from the huge lock gates. Adrenalin was crackling all round'.

What are you working for? We are not usually clear about what we want and what makes us happy. If our work isn't much fun, we may say it is the means to an end - but what is the end we are working for, and when will we achieve it? We may strive for money and status, thinking this will bring us happiness – but will they? When should we consider alternatives to work, and how can we check them out before we commit ourselves? If we or our partner is not enjoying working life very much, what can we do about it?

Years ago I was driving on the M25 motorway around London, on the way to a conference on a Sunday evening, and I realised that I had all the income I needed. That is not to say that if I were given more I would not spend it, but rather that I could be happy on this income, *provided I could choose what I wanted to do.*

Fast forward to a time when I was in a plane very early on a Monday morning looking down at the Channel beneath, seeing a few tiny yachts and realizing that if I stopped work for a year or two, and rented out our house, I could manage to have more or less the income (allowing for inflation) I had decided I needed all those years before on the M25. So why was I working and not on those yachts?

Things seldom happen quickly, and it was a few more years before I was able to do anything about it, partly because our son James was still at school, and partly because it's as well to give such matters not just one thought but two or three and then some more, but my wife Nicky was supportive, and over time I was able to develop a practical idea of how we might do this, and I was finally able to look up from the deck of our yacht 'Intrepid of Dover', at the tiny specks of planes overhead, and wonder what the people in the planes were thinking.

And later, as I was sailing in the Pacific, miles from anywhere, landing a fish or adjusting the sails, or avoiding a gale, I wondered why more people didn't do this, or whatever their dream is.

Tempting though it was to stay in the Pacific, we sailed around, 50,000 miles in all, and I had the chance to investigate some more of the psychology of happiness and what factors are important in helping us make the best decisions to achieve a good work life balance. Then I returned to work to check out how practical this is, even if we have been away for 5 years or more. This book is the result, with some brief extracts from our sailing log as we sailed around the world. I have put these in a border beneath the Chapter headings.

Suppose we are trying to decide whether we or our partner should change job, and possibly stop work altogether. This is clearly a very big decision, not to be taken lightly, and if it were a financial decision like whether to buy a house or a car or a pension, or make an investment, we would do a considerable amount of research on it, comparing the alternatives. But suppose we want to get a happier and more contented life. This is more complicated, but it is increasingly what people are asking for, so it is a reasonable objective. Indeed, it is even in the US Declaration of Independence as a right, 'the pursuit of happiness':

> 'We hold these truths to be self-evident, that all men are created equal, that they are endowed by their Creator with certain unalienable Rights, that among these are Life, Liberty and the pursuit of Happiness...That to secure these rights, Governments are instituted among Men, deriving their just powers from the consent of the governed...'
>
> Declaration of Independence drafted by Thomas Jefferson 11 – 28 June 1776.

What should we do to get a happier, more contented life, a better work life balance? This is not academic; it is intensely practical. Finance will play a part in this, but there is much more to it than that. Otherwise we will just go down a blind alley of endlessly looking for more money.

We could try out a few of the opportunities that we can think of – but this would be like trying to cure an illness by randomly taking medicines, or making random investments. Better, we could try to think what made us happy in the past. But what made us happy when we were 16 (for example) is unlikely to make us happy now even if it were practical, because we and the world have changed since then. And anyway (as we shall see) our memory of when we were 16 is likely to be inaccurate.

Or we could find out what made other people in similar situations to us happier, and by how much. This is Positive Psychology, or the Psychology of Happiness. What works for other people will not necessarily work for us, but it is a reasonable place to start, along with what has made us happy in the past.

This will help us to decide whether to focus on getting more money and how much, or starting a new business or three, or buying a more attractive house or second house, faster status car or new partner or lots of friends, or a big screen TV or a satisfying or high status job or helping others, or other activities, or working part time, or taking a sabbatical, or extended time off, or getting secondment to a charity. Until recently there was very little evidence on this, and our pursuit of happiness would have been hit or miss, a wander through life. But there is increasing evidence on happiness now, and it is common sense to consider it. Indeed, NOT to have explored what makes people happy is to risk making lots of poor decisions about our life.

Like most psychology research, the results are sometimes unclear, the experiments are sometimes artificial and it is often not clear what is cause and effect. For example, when we find that married people seem to be slightly happier than single people, is this because marriage makes people happier or because happy people are more likely to get married? And what difference does it make who we marry? This is explored in Chapter 7. We may think we are good at making decisions about our life, but there are a number of traps, and the psychology of happiness has something to say about this as well. I have tried to keep it straightforward, avoiding too many ifs and buts; however, the evidence is not always clear, and you need to be aware of this.

There is even the nagging doubt that if we focus on Happiness then we may not actually end up happier. Maybe the best way to pursue happiness is to ignore it altogether, and get on with other things that we find interesting and fulfilling. Then happiness may come along as an unintended consequence that is nonetheless welcome. This is discussed in Chapter 20.

Measuring happiness sounds strange, but is quite straightforward. Surveys ask people 'Taking all things together, how would you say things are these days – would you say that you are very happy, pretty happy, or not too happy? Or 'How satisfied are you with your life as a whole these days? Are you very satisfied, satisfied, not very satisfied, or not at all satisfied?'

Questions like these are strongly influenced by our mood at the time we are answering, and we may even give a different answer one hour later. So we have to treat all these measurements carefully. However, if the studies are properly managed, they can give us insights into what causes happiness and how we might best and most effectively pursue it.

This research can involve endless debates over the definition of happiness. Philosophers and religions have been debating this for as long as people have been able to speak. So getting tied up in more debates about the definition of happiness is not productive. Most of us have a good idea of what happiness is, and whether we are happy or not at any moment in time.

However, there is a distinction that you may want to think about. Is happiness:

1. **Excitement and Enjoying** – actively seeking out fun things and pleasurable events and achieving goals, needing continual novelty

AND/OR:

2. **Contentment** – satisfied, peace of mind, secure, not being unhappy, enjoying things as they are, not too much, not too little, enjoying the journey

Different people relate more to one than the other, and we will see in the Chapter on Personality that this distinction relates to two powerful personality dimensions and two different brain mechanisms. It may be that *both* Excitement *and* Contentment are required for what we might call long-lasting happiness. From my own survey it does appear that as people get older, contentment becomes more important. But for now I will use the overall term happiness.

I will also consider finance. Most financial advisors start by asking what income we want – but this depends on lifestyle, and what age and family circumstance we are in, so what lifestyle we want over the next 5-10 years is really the key question. We should not allow choices on our lifestyle to be made for us by someone who is only qualified in financial affairs. That would be like asking a garage mechanic to advise us on our health for example.

Intrepid of Dover beating to windward British Virgin Islands
2016

2. The Relationship between Money and Happiness; Minimum Income; Wealth as a Vaccine

> In Natalei village, Fiji, people told us that they did not want a full money economy - they had enough land to grow all the food they needed, wood and palms for houses, clean water, and the stress of finding enough money for the few items that required money, made them realise that actually they preferred village life with less money and less stress, to more money, possessions and stress.

Too many of us jump to the conclusion that we don't have enough money to do what we really want, so work longer than we need until ill health prevents us from ever doing it.

For example, sailing can be expensive yet we met people of all stages of wealth from multi-millionaires to engineers, welders or vets who had next to no money yet frequently seemed happier than those with massive wealth. Money, provided we have enough, is less important than we think provided we are doing what we want.

So a key question for us is 'How much income do we need to be happy most of the time?' Only we can answer this for ourselves but there are some clues. Some of these relate to things within our control, others Government can do something about (and we can influence them by who we vote for):

A. Increasing average income in a country does not increase average happiness, provided the income is above a minimum level.

B. Wealth and higher income help protect against depression

C. Having a higher income increases the chance a person will be happy, but this is often counterbalanced by other effects.

A. Higher income and happiness

In Britain and the USA average incomes/household increased significantly in real terms, and average real income/person of working age has doubled since 1945. But in Britain and the USA only 30% of people say they are very happy – the same now as in 1945 ie higher income is not making people as a whole any happier. Data on income and happiness are affected by inflation, exchange rates, and political and social events in the country in question, so figures need to be treated with caution. On a country level, as a generalization, provided average income/person is above about $24,000 or £18,000/year, increases in income in any country (eg pay rises, tax breaks, and higher allowances) do not generally make the population any happier. It would seem that above $24,000 or £18,000/year/person we need as a country to look for things other than income to increase our happiness.

To see where we fit in, average full time earnings in UK in 2015 were £26,000/year. In the public sector average earnings were about £26,000/year, and in Financial and Business Services £33,000/year. The top 10% of workers earned more than £54,000/year, the median (average) earned £27,000/year, and the lowest paid 10% earned less than £15,000/year. Full time men earned on average £30,000/year, full time women earned £25,000/year on average.

To give a historical perspective, and to illustrate full and part time work, and the effect of the 2007/8 Financial crisis, earnings in the UK in 2007 were:

Before Tax Income in the UK

	2007 Full Time	2007 Part Time
Lowest 10% of Men earned less than	£14,000	£2,000
Median Men (ie 50%)	£26,000	£7,000
Top 10% of Men earned more than	£52,000	£21,000
Lowest 10% of Women earned less than	£12,000	£3,000
Median Women (ie 50%)	£20,000	£8,000
Top 10% of Women earned more than	£39,000	£17,000

Workers on adult rates whose pay was not affected by absence. Figures rounded to nearest £1000. Source UK National Statistics

In the 8 years from 2007 to 2015, average earnings have increased marginally, and there have been changes in full/part time work, and gender equality. In 2015 the average household income was £25,000 for retired households, and £34,000 for non-retired households, with the overall average £31,000/year. However, people are not much happier, indeed from 2005 to 2010, overall happiness changed not at all.

To politicians and to us, this is disappointing – all that extra income and development and we are no happier than when we started? We need to know why this is if we are to get a good idea of how much income we need.

This may be because of:

1. Changes in what we do to get that income and what we spend it on, like hours worked, house prices etc
2. Community issues like family break-up, crime, drugs and debt
3. Increased expectations, stress and greater inequality
4. An increase in the quality of 'normal' goods and services so there is less gain from luxury goods or services
5. Averages for the population do not necessarily apply to us as individuals

Higher income may involve greater stress. £18,000($24,000/year) may only provide sufficient goods and services for a lifestyle that is happy and contented, if we do not focus on having more than our neighbours. If we decide we need more, the extra effort, inconvenience and stress caused by extra hours worked or greater work intensity to achieve the real increase in household income may be causing unhappiness which is cancelling out any gain in average happiness.

If we already earn more than the £18,000/$24,000/year, then a reduction of income may cause unhappiness – but as we shall see, the effect may not be great, (some studies indicate a 3% drop in happiness) and we will probably adapt to it, and may even gain happiness because of less stress, shorter hours, greater personal control etc.

But we are individuals not averages. What happens to individuals whose income is above £18,000/year if they receive a significant pay rise, say 30%? The overall increase in happiness is only about 3%. Work is a deal – hours and effort in exchange for income and benefits. If income is increased but effort and stress required increased even more, then the net effect is likely to be unhappiness, not happiness.

Hours of work in Western countries/worker do not seem on average to have increased very much during the time that real incomes were rising, so this is not the whole explanation. However, greater inequality; and increased numbers of mothers working are factors, (because they may work part time or fewer hours even if full time, and these dual roles can be very stressful). Rising inequality in income causes significant stress, as the visibility of those with high incomes increases the demands on those with lower incomes.

We may feel it is right to work more hours to get a higher income. Unfortunately for the workaholic, valuing high income, status, material goods etc has no connection with actual income, and goes with less happiness. In other words, wanting a higher income is unlikely in itself to achieve it, and may actually make us unhappier. What makes us happy is usually not purchasable, so any extra income buys goods but these don't make us happy, they just stack up in the garage or are sold on Ebay.

In the USA people were asked what the most important things in life were. 50% said family and friends, 20% said religious faith and spirituality, only 4% said monetary success. So even the prime capitalist country does not regard money as most important!

In the UK, 10% say that their ambition is to be rich, but 60% say that they prefer a situation where they have 'enough money to be free of financial worries'. This may be awareness that being rich is not the goal, and we become bored with material things and alternatives to them become much more attractive. Celebrities when they have acquired wealth, often turn to alternative life-styles and values.

So it is not just standard of living that makes us happy. Try comparing your own standard of living now compared to the richest person in the world even 200 years ago. Now we can travel to distant countries in a few hours, we have instant entertainment and quality music in our own home, we have bright light during night time hours, our health is better, our homes are more comfortable, and we have massive libraries of information available instantaneously. A King might well swap his palace then for our life style now. So why aren't we happier?

We only had to see the faces of the owner of the largest yacht in the bay when a larger yacht came in (and there always was a bigger one) to see the answer to this. If your happiness depends on having something more or better or longer or more expensive than others the only way you will manage this is to associate with people who don't have nearly as much as you. And funnily enough this is a very good strategy, but not one that many people adopt. But higher income does have some positive effects:

B. High income and wealth as a 'vaccine' against depression

Wealth does seem to protect against unhappiness and depression – at least to some extent. In the USA 9% of the top quarter of income earners are unhappy, compared to 14% of the lowest quarter. In the UK, 6% of the top quarter of income earners report being unhappy whereas 12% of the lowest quarter do. So should we aim to be in the top quarter of incomes to reduce our chance of being very unhappy?

This is important because depression appears to be increasing in frequency even as real incomes are increasing. In the 1960's about 2% of Americans had experienced major depression at some point before age 35; now the comparable figure is closer to 15%. And this is in spite of new drugs, counselling therapists, and increasing incomes. It almost seems that instead of trying to be happy we should focus on avoiding unhappiness.

Maybe increasing wealth and incomes are causing depression, but:

a. we may be recognizing that someone is depressed, whereas previously we might have ignored them; and

b. it is increasingly possible to 'cure' depression, the most effective treatment being a combination of anti-depressant drugs and counselling either by a therapist or a friend or relative.

Nonetheless depression can be devastating, and can totally incapacitate someone, making it impossible for them to work or sometimes to do anything. And there is increasing acceptance that this is an illness – albeit one that like many others is at least partially caused by the environment in which we live and work.

How does wealth or higher income protect against depression? When something breaks on a house, or car or boat or even a person (something always does), we either have to use skill or money to fix it. If we are short of money and don't have the skill then the impact of the breakage will constitute a major worry, and we will certainly feel that we are out of control of the situation. However, if we have enough wealth or income, then we know we will probably be able to fix the problem quickly and don't need to get stressed about it. This also means that we can be confident and take more risks because we know that if something does go wrong it can be fixed. This may be why most people rate security as being the most important aspect of money.

Certainly we saw a reasonable proportion of people sailing who became over-stressed and depressed when things broke because they didn't have much money and focused on the loss, even though they were by no means poor.

Clearly this is not 100% effective (few cures are). Happiness is affected more by relationships than by money, as we shall see. We have only to read the gossip pages, (or increasingly the business pages) to learn how some very rich or high earner has been depressed; and anyway we have already seen that 6-9% of the top quarter of income earners report being unhappy (which is not the same as being depressed, but may lead to it).

There are some countries (eg Korea, Taiwan, Puerto Rico) where duty and close family ties rather than high income seems to be the main factor countering depression. Although income/head is not very high in these countries (although increasing), rates of depression are low. So culture is also important.

C. Higher income increases our chances to be happy

A high income relative to the average gives us a greater chance to be happy or even very happy. Recall that the average number of people in USA and UK who rated themselves as very happy has stayed constant at 30%? Well, 45% of people with incomes in the top quarter were very happy in the USA, in Britain it is 40%. A 40-45% chance of being very happy! This is worth striving for – indeed it may well be what motivates many people.

But the way this works is complex, and some studies show that most of the effect is caused by factors that tend to go with higher income – like higher status, better health etc, and income by itself is almost irrelevant. Nonetheless higher income has an attraction as something we can (usually) do something about. But the effort we put in to increase our income may have other unintended side effects like stress which lowers our happiness and that of others around us. This is explored in Chapter 3. And as incomes generally increase, so the goalposts keep moving – the income required to be in the top quarter goes up.

Higher income may make people happier by:

- enabling them to spend more time enjoying themselves and less time worrying about how to save money;
- enabling a greater sense of trust – half of high income earners in all but the smallest communities felt able to trust people, as compared to 30% for everyone else (including the high income earners in the smallest communities);
- acting as the vaccine we talked about, cushioning them against risks;
- giving a feeling of high self-esteem or status.

So if we are considering whether to change job or stop full time work altogether, we need to investigate carefully the income we think we need in the future.

Intrepid of Dover beating to windward British Virgin Islands
2016

3. Change of Work and Income

> The 'roads' in the Tuamotu atolls are sand, the policier doubles up as the mayor, the 3 small shops open when they please, and a wonderful woman (called by everyone grandmere) bakes bread and melt in your mouth pain au chocolat for the whole island.

Imagine someone who has an introvert personality, (so tends to avoid meeting people, is less outgoing, does not take risks meeting strangers etc) in the job of a sales executive whose job it is to persuade strangers to buy their firm's products.

Or someone who is naturally very anxious and worried in a job which involves frequent deadlines and decisions with very little tolerance and severe consequences if they are wrong.

Or someone who is naturally an extravert in a job which involves entering data into a computer all day.

All 3 of these people are likely to be less happy than they might otherwise be, because their job is taking up half or so of their waking hours and as a result of their choice of job, their personality is being continually challenged to do things that do not come naturally to them. As one psychologist put it, 'their psychological immune system has to work very hard to keep them happy'. (Gilbert).

Why did these 3 people end up in these jobs, since they probably knew that their natural personality was not well suited to these jobs? The likelihood is that given a totally free choice, they would have chosen something different. But life is never that simple. Suppose the sales job was the only one available at the time, or within a reasonable distance of where they lived, or which provided part time work, so they can look after children or an elderly relative, or simply pays more money than other jobs, and the money is desperately needed to pay off mortgage bills. And once in a job there is tremendous inertia to stay. There are many graduates who have taken a 'temporary' job after graduating and find themselves still in the organisation 3 years later with significant often negative implications for their career.

Or they may have done well in an organization because of their attention to detail and ability to avoid being distracted. Then they are promoted to a position, perhaps head of a section where they have to interact with staff they do not know well, customers and potential customers, and to seek out and meet people they have never met before as potential customers or investors or bankers.

All of us may conclude that a job which pays more money must be better for us, and more likely to make us happy, and that for others around us (our family and others who depend on us) it is necessary for us to take the higher paying job. We may also reason that if we can just stick the job for a period of time and accumulate wealth then we will be able to change jobs or even stop altogether.

The organization may have fallen into the trap of promoting the best performing employee on the criteria for their present job, and put them in a role which requires a different set of skills. Now it may be that the knowledge and determination they bring to the new job is sufficient to offset any lack of natural skill or (for example) a tendency to avoid people. And from their point of view, the extra income certainly in the short term is likely to bring happiness and contentment. But over time there is likely to be increasing stress and unhappiness as the demands of the job clash with their natural personality.

Whether we are happy in a job will be influenced by what we have to deal with – we will pay particular attention to those aspects that we find difficult, and may imagine other jobs or roles which do not place these same requirements on us. We will also adapt over time to any extra income and status, so that this has less positive effect on our happiness.

When people are struggling in their work they tend to repeat but even harder, the behaviour that they found to be successful in previous jobs – even though this may have little relevance to the challenge facing them. So for example, if we were promoted from our previous job where analysis and attention to detail was the key to success, when we are struggling, we are likely to drop back on even more analysis and striving for attention to detail – even if the task actually requires more people skills and strategic vision.

This means that there will come a time when a change of job is likely to increase our happiness (or decrease our unhappiness). And even if our income would reduce as a result of the change, we may still be happier because the influence of income on happiness is only about 3%.

There are 3 issues we have to balance here. One is income; the second is relative income (when we compare our income with others around us); the third is control over our lives. They are related. The first 2 are considered in this Chapter, control is considered in the next.

Income

If we compare high middle and low incomes, whilst there is some effect on happiness, it is not very great, so taking a new role just because the pay is a bit more, or rejecting it because the income is a bit less is not sensible by itself.

Satisfaction with life from 10 (Satisfied) to 1 (Dissatisfied) by Household Income Level UK

Happiness	Lowest 1/3 Income	Middle 1/3 Income	Highest 1/3 Income
9,10	28%	27%	32%
7,8	38%	46%	47%
5,6	22%	22%	13%
3,4	9%	5%	3%
1,2	4%	1%	4%

World Values Survey 1999 (% rounded to nearest whole number)

The equivalent figures for USA using the same question are:

Happiness	Lowest 1/3 Income	Middle 1/3 Income	Highest 1/3 Income
9,10	30%	36%	41%
7,8	42%	43%	49%
5,6	19%	16%	9%
3,4	6%	5%	1%
1,2	3%	0%	0%

World Values Survey (% rounded to nearest whole number)

91% of the lowest income band in the USA are fairly or very happy, (rating 5 or above) and 87% in the UK. So clearly high income is not necessary for happiness, although it makes it a bit more likely as we established in Chapter 2.

On the other hand, rates of serious depression are increasing in the developed world at the same time as rates of divorce, family separation, one parent families, victims of crime, and people living by themselves have all risen significantly. These are people who are likely to figure in the dissatisfied ratings of 1,2 and 3,4 in the lowest 1/3 income. In the USA these make up 9% of the lowest 1/3 band, compared to 1% for the highest 1/3 band; and in the UK 13% against 7% in the highest income band.

So it is possible that extra income does make us happier – it is just that there are so many other factors working to make us unhappier, like stress, inequality, status envy, crime, separation, drugs, etc. that they cancel out the effect of higher income.

This is important because whereas we can influence to a significant extent the work we do and when we stop and hence our income, we can do little about the rates of crime and drug use, income inequality and family disintegration in the country we live in apart from emigrating or living abroad or even moving from inner city to the countryside. The corrosive effect of inequality is analysed clearly by Wilkinson and Pickett in 'The Spirit Level'.

Happiness has not increased in the USA over the last 40 years partly because median real incomes for white males in the USA has hardly changed at all from 1960's to 2000's (roughly $40,000/year in $'s applicable in 2000). There has been an increase in inequality, with the top quartile increasing their income significantly in real terms, but since these people were already reasonably happy it has not affected *average* happiness much, and as we have seen there has been an increase in depression generally probably caused by the greater inequality.

Real incomes for white households with both man and wife working has increased from $45,000 (1960's) to $70,000 (2000's), but this has required more hours worked and more stress and although some prices have fallen, the price of houses has risen dramatically even with the latest fall, so the overall money left after necessities may not be much more at all.

What we are seeing is a transfer of money from young workers (with massive mortgages or rents) to older house owners, who then have to use the significantly increased value of their property to pay for care in old age that in the past they would not have needed because they often would not have lived so long and if they did, their children would have looked after them. When this older generation die at 80+, the money is transferred by inheritance back to their children at age 60+ when they are often too old to enjoy it as much, and the main beneficiary is the government which taxes the higher incomes generated by 2 worker households, and then taxes the inheritance on transfer at death. If we really are pursuing happiness, we have not found a very effective way of doing it.

The income of black families in the USA where the wife does not work has increased from about $20,000/household (1960's) to about $30,000/household (2000's), but this is still well below the 'minimum' for happiness of $24,000/head. Black families where both partners work have increased their income from about $35,000 (1960's) to about $60,000 (2000's) so this has been a real improvement, but only about 1/3 of black families fits this description. Only 15% of black households have a man breadwinner, whereas in 45% a woman is the sole earner. There are increasing strains on these households, and there is even some evidence that in the 2000's black middle classes are slipping back relatively. In other words, the lack of an increase in happiness at the same time as average real incomes have almost doubled may not be so surprising when we delve into the figures.

What do we spend extra money on?

Imagine we receive a big increase in salary, which is partly offset by extra tax; and the rest of which we put towards our pension. The net effect of this increase on our quality of life is therefore – nothing. Of course, we may feel better because we are building up a bigger pension for when we retire. We may even by some stretch of the imagination be pleased with ourselves for our tax contribution to the Government and its spending on good causes like schools and health. But in the day to day run of things this is unlikely to significantly affect our level of happiness.

We could alternatively use the extra income to get a bigger mortgage and buy a bigger house or car or yacht. This would have the advantage of being much more obvious – as we wake up in the morning or come home at night, we would see the physical reality of the house, and presumably experience more happiness – at least initially until we adapt to it. This may even be why house prices in the USA, UK and developed countries increased so much 1960-2006 (with some small variations). The effect of a pay rise will depend on what it is spent on. And the higher our income, the more choice we have how to spend it:

At one time I was responsible for pay in an important Middle Eastern country. We divided income into:

    A. Spendable Income – this covers 'essentials' - everything you 'need' to spend including food, every day clothes, transport etc.

    B. Discretionary Income – this is the amount left over after you have provided for the 'essentials' of life.

    C. Incentives – to encourage you to stay in a job which is stressful (difficult location or long hours).

    D. Bonuses – to reinforce and reward high achievement and share the profits of the organisation.

What the experts find is that spendable income (A) increases quite slowly even as pay goes up significantly. A high income earner spends little extra on food or transport compared to someone on half of what they are earning. So increases in pay tend to increase discretionary income by a much greater proportion thereby giving more choice in what we do with our money. Incentives and Bonuses further add to this. So what do we spend this discretionary income on?

In the USA about 25% of total spending by middle classes is used to try to signal status ie deliberately buying a higher priced status good when a cheaper one that is equally good exists. However, CEO pay has massively increased as a proportion of average earnings, from 40 times in 1960's to 500 times in 2000's, so the middle classes are never going to catch up.

This is offset to some extent by redistributive taxation – higher rates on higher incomes; and adaptation (we redefine upwards what we think we 'need') – but the effect is still the same – if our income is already fairly high, we will have more discretion on how to spend any extra, but it gets more and more difficult to find ways to spend it which increase happiness.

Relative Income

Relative Income has a bigger effect than Absolute Pay. We may be pleased to receive an increase in salary, but if everyone gets the same increase, then we will only be about 1/3 as happy as if we alone got the increase. This is strange – after all the fact that others have also had good fortune should make us also happier – and in any case their good fortune does not in any way hinder us from spending our increase in any way we wish to.

Worse, as we get used to the extra income and adapt to it, after a year or less the happiness caused by the extra income has largely disappeared even though the income is still coming in month after month – and that's not even mentioning inflation. So when we are considering whether to move to a new higher paying job, we need to be aware that we will adapt to the new income, and if we start to compare ourselves with a new higher paid set of colleagues, our happiness is likely to disappear even faster.

Even a 30% increase in income is eaten away by the perception that we need still more. Each year we come to rely on this extra income, and it seems that only income over and above that which we expect and think we need, makes us happy or very happy. People were asked 'What is the smallest amount of money that a family of 4 needs to get along in this community?' Their answers seemed to be based on the average income around them, so that as real incomes rise in the community, so the perceived *smallest* amount of income needed also rises. We may try to 'store' extra income in wealth, investments or material possessions like property or cars, but we can never have again the time we used to get the income. And anyway once we have enough, more of something does not make us happier.

This even happens in a more general sense. In East Germany following reunification, salaries increased significantly – but people started to compare themselves with colleagues in West Germany, and overall levels of happiness did not increase. In many countries women are increasingly getting jobs which pay much better than before, but are now comparing themselves with men in these higher paying jobs, rather than lower paid women. This results in women being on average no happier than before, because they have changed who they compare themselves to, (their reference group).

Suppose we are considering a decrease in income, perhaps by working fewer hours, or moving to a less stressful job, or stopping altogether? Provided we stay above the $24,000, £18,000/person/year income level, there may be only a small reduction in happiness (perhaps 3%) due to pay. But what about relative income? If we still compare ourselves with the people we did previously, then our relative income will have dropped, and this will reduce our happiness, even after allowing for the effect of the absolute reduction in income.

This will be exaggerated by another effect explored in Chapter 15 - we like winning but we dislike losing things even more. In fact, we are likely to regard a drop in income of say £5,000/year as twice as bad (or unhappiness causing) as an increase of £5,000 is happiness inducing. This will be particularly so if there are some high profile obvious items or events that we will lose, like a company car, or the status that goes with being able to invite people to events. So we can predict that a drop in our income *if we continue to compare ourselves with the same people we used to*, is likely to have a significant downward effect on our happiness – even if our income stays well above the $24,000/£18,000/head threshold. We will adapt to this (probably by stopping comparing ourselves with previous colleagues) but we may lose friends by doing so, and if not our happiness is likely to be significantly reduced.

But there is an even more powerful effect – Personal Control. This is explored in the next Chapter.

Customs Officials on Intrepid, Port Blair, Andaman Islands,
Indian Ocean 2007

4. Personal Control, Commitment, Superstition, Shopping and Choice

> I asked David, a villager: "Would you prefer to live here in Erromango, (a small island in mid Pacific), or in the West?" He replied (in pidgin English): "I prefer to live here, because I can do what I like, when I like, and talk to my friends; in the West, I think time is money and you always have to do things for other people. So even though I would have money and trucks and everything else I would not be able to enjoy them as much because my time would be controlled by others, so I prefer to live here."

Personal Control has a major impact on Happiness. When British people in the professions, doctors, lawyers, senior business people, those in high status jobs and their spouses were asked for their reaction to the statement 'I feel in control of my life', 96% agreed. 90% of them also agreed that 'I usually get what I want out of life'. This is worth bearing in mind when we are trying to decide on a career, and what to do next.

By contrast only 61% of labourers and similar occupations get what they want out of life, and 81% feel they have control of their life. This is not bad, and probably reflects the benefits of living in a developed country; poor countries have a lower percentage of people agreeing with these statements.

In UK many of the unhappiest people come from the lowest Social Class, even though their income may be above £18,000/year. Low social class and status can cause unhappiness and depression. The mechanism may often be low control.

The importance of personal control becomes particularly clear when labourers in the lowest quarter of income earners who nonetheless report high personal control, are compared with those in the top quarter of income earners who have relatively low personal control of their life.

The labourers who had high personal control rated their happiness at an average of 7.9 out of 10, whereas those in the top quarter of income earners who had low personal control gave themselves only 5.8 out of 10 for happiness. In other words, personal control seems to be more important than social class and pay. Happiness is largely influenced by personal control – and indeed when we compare countries where personal control is limited (as in communist countries) happiness is generally low.

Social Class by itself seems to have a medium-low influence on happiness, partly because there are more opportunities for greater personal control at higher Social Groups. Attractiveness or celebrity status may be thought of as similar to social class, and also gives us greater personal control – the ability to get things done. Changes in perceived attractiveness or celebrity status may therefore have a marked effect on happiness for this reason if no other.

> The feeling of having personal control over our life is a very much better predictor of happiness than income. Twenty times as big an influence in fact by one estimate.

The significant effect of personal control on happiness is important when we decide what to do about a new job or whether to downsize or stop work- or even to marry, live together, separate or divorce. If we continue in a job in which we do not feel we have much control, we may continue to have a high income. Our happiness will therefore be medium at best, because our income, though high, is likely to be similar to others, and the low personal control is likely to make us unhappy.

However, if we change to another job with more personal control or stop working for an organisation altogether, (for example by doing something we really want to do, and/or by contracting or free-lancing), then our income will probably fall, (it may increase), but we will adapt to this by shifting the comparison point to new colleagues; and the increase in personal control will probably have a significantly greater increase on happiness than the loss of income.

Personal control today is not much use if we anticipate we will be out of control tomorrow. The most favoured aspect of money is security. Wealth, status, contacts, skills and even 'favours' may be seen as ways to store resources for personal control in the future.

Redundancy

If we are made redundant, this is clear loss of personal control as regards work, and being made unemployed often produces significant unhappiness, and can lead to depression. There is even some evidence from Australia that it is the most motivated of those looking for a new job who gets most depressed, perhaps because the strenuous job seeking emphasises the obvious lack of control.

However, there can be too much personal control. Shopkeepers and small business-people who are largely in personal control of their business are less happy than people in large organisations that pay about the same; and managers are more anxious about their future than professionals.

So it is not all plain sailing. If the change of job and reduction of income means that we have to concentrate on activities to save money or to earn enough to live reasonably on, then the feeling of personal control may be illusory. Although in theory an unemployed person is free to do what they want, a low income means that in practice they do not normally have the means to do it, and so they would not easily be described as being in control of their lives. This has clear relevance if we are deciding whether we are happy at work or whether we would rather stop.

Becoming unemployed indeed causes a 6% reduction in happiness. This may also explain why a minimum of £18,000/person seems to be important for happiness in a country. Above this level people generally can feel in control of their lives; whereas below this they are largely struggling with circumstances beyond their control to just survive. This even affects children; families of the unemployed in Finland suffered from more disorders, and were admitted to hospital more often than families of the employed.

The free-enterprise market driven consumer economy we have now is a very efficient way to give people personal control. This is because the market, acting through price setting enables we consumers to indicate what we prefer, what we want and do not want, and even what makes us happy, and by how much. This is increasingly prevalent as more and more of our daily life is based on money from access to clubs, sports events or parties, status, social networking, customer relationships, hiring a celebrity to open a fete or party, or even customer loyalty. On the other hand, if we lived in a communist regime, we would notice the lack of empowerment – indeed this and the consequent lack of feedback is probably the main cause for the collapse of most of them. We may complain that advertising and consumerism reduce our personal control, but if this is unhappiness, try living in a communist command driven economy.

Some people even propose that our main aim is to increase our control over our life. This is particularly the case in western societies where the focus is on the individual and the passionate call for 'Less Government, No New Taxes' in the USA reflects this. One of the best predictors of whether people will vote is a strong belief in personal control.

Personal control in other words includes a belief that we can influence events, choose amongst outcomes, cope with the results, and understand why they happened.

Commitments and saying No

Personal control is more than a belief – it means the real ability to influence events that are important to us. And this means being able to say 'No' as well as 'Yes'. So personal control is not just doing what we want. It means exactly what it implies, that we control our behaviour, we develop habits that help us to achieve our goals, and sometimes we make commitments to voluntarily control our behaviour. So for example personal control means we do not just eat whatever looks attractive whenever we want it.

This is the ability to 'delay gratification'. In other words, to decide to wait rather than to enjoy all the good things all at once. This was illustrated neatly with children who were shown a scrumptious donut and told that if they waited 5 minutes they could eat this and another one. Some children were able to wait, (often by distracting themselves eg playing, looking at something else etc) and years later were found to be more successful in business and have higher incomes than the children who could not wait and ate the scrumptious donut straight away. Depressed people often have trouble delaying gratification and feel powerless.

We learn much of our approach to personal control and how we relate to people from our parents. Children of businessmen help other children only when they received something back in return, but the children of bureaucrats helped others because they thought that this was the right thing to do. Children whose parents' job requires obedience are taught to value obedience whereas if the parents' job requires critical thinking and being in control, they teach their children the importance of critical thinking and personal control.

The search for happiness (or the relief of unhappiness) through eating is a good example of our mistaken thinking about how to be happy. If we feel powerless or downtrodden at work we may compensate by eating, which we can control. There may also be a cultural status effect – in some societies, fat people are high status, so people may believe consciously or not, that eating more gives higher status. Overuse of alcohol is another example (although moderate alcohol does make people happier for a time).

Many of our social conventions such as marriage, thrift, hard work, laws prohibiting theft, corruption, etc are ways to encourage people who could do things that might harm themselves and others, to take a prudent attitude and delay the gratification that a quick fix or fling or laziness or corruption might bring. They are designed to increase the happiness of everyone in the long term, even though individuals may find them frustrating in the short term. One of the main determinants of happiness in countries seems to be a set of laws and conventions that empowers citizens, but then induces self-control through social conventions. One reason for the leveling off of happiness in Western countries despite huge increases in income, may be the weakening of these conventions and inducements to self-control. Whereas before lack of money restricted choice, now the only limit is often our sense of personal control.

Greater knowledge about what causes happiness and unhappiness is critical to give us greater personal control precisely because the old social conventions are weakening, and we have to chart our own course in these turbulent times. Knowing the main causes can help us to reconsider our own set of values, and decide how to develop our lives at work and at leisure.

This of course imposes a considerable burden on each individual – instead of social norms controlling our behaviour (like marriage controlling sexual behaviour, rigid work discipline, church exhortations on the value of hard work and thrift etc) we have to work it out for ourselves

Superstitions

When we really want something but can't control it, we often create explanations and even act on them in a vain attempt to gain control. These are superstitions or self-fulfilling prophecies. They can lead us to make poor judgments about work and elsewhere, and it is therefore important to be aware of how they work.

For example, we know that a roulette wheel or lottery draw is random, but think that when we bet on our lucky numbers we win. Or when we carry a particular charm, or (as I heard today) visit a particular pub or watch the game in person, our team always wins. Even following fashion in clothes or diets can fit this pattern. ('I wore the latest fashion and gained a promotion'). The cause may well be personality not the clothes, but the explanation says that it is, and is likely to encourage subsequent buying of new fashions.

Superstitions start when some behaviour is followed by a good event. We maybe repeat the behaviour and perhaps our team wins again or we are given a bonus. We repeat this again, and if we score (in either sense), we probably have generated a superstition. On the occasions when it doesn't work, we are likely to find it easier to fine tune the superstition (it only works on home games for example or only clothes from this designer); than to discard it. Our search for personal control is so strong that it can lead us into irrational superstitions. Some people believe that religions are a search for a feeling of control.

Learned Helplessness

If we are genuinely not in personal control of events affecting us, we may experience 'learned helplessness'. This can be a major cause of depression in individuals at work and at home; and sports psychologists work hard to counter this in teams that are losing. Conversely, leadership may be little more than helping people to have faith in their ability to achieve. We are prone to look for evidence of personal control or lack of it in others, and then respond accordingly. So if we see a person struggling with a problem, we may think that our chances of solving it are also low – and this is exactly what happens when we are in groups.

The explanations we create for ourselves about success and failure seem to be very important – because they have the potential to make us happy or depressed. In particular how we explain events in terms of personal control - whether we think that the cause of events is internal (we caused it) or external (some outside event caused it); and one-off (specific) or general (it will always happen). If we explain success in terms that we caused it to happen, and it will happen again (internal, general) then we are likely to perceive our personal control as high, and our happiness with life will increase. On the other hand if we think success is because of external factors, and one-off then we may be more inclined to regard it as a 'flash in the pan' and almost superstitiously look for the next event to be a failure. This outlook is more likely to lead to depression, or at least to low levels of self-esteem and happiness. This is explored later.

Personal Control and Shopping

One example of personal control is the desirability of high performance cars or motorbikes to middle aged and older people who almost never drive them at even a fraction of what they are designed for. So why buy them? It seems that people often buy them because they want the feeling that if they wanted to they could do 140mph, and beat every car on the road. Knowing they could do this is enough to yield happiness (and possibly status); it may also help them to hang onto their self-image as a young adventurer.

People sometimes talk of 'Retail Therapy' ie shopping to get over a mild depression. There may be more to this than meets the eye, in that shops are some of the best places to feel in control, provided we choose the shops we go into and what we shop for. We exchange money for a feeling of personal control and companionship – we can choose what we want, change our mind; ask the sales-person to bring something else, and she will still smile at us and do as we ask. Personal shoppers take this exchange to new heights, and 'shopaholics' are saying something about their inner feelings. Of course if we go to shops where we don't have enough money to buy anything, we will rediscover a sense of powerlessness. Which may be one reason why coffee bars like Starbucks are so popular – we know we can buy anything they sell, so get a feeling of power along with the latte. Credit cards do something similar (until they max out).

What percent of your time do you spend shopping? 5%, 10%, 20%? Consumer psychologists have found that women spend about 4% of their time shopping, men about 2%. But 93% of American teenage girls rated shopping as their preferred activity, older women also like shopping. Upper class women like exciting displays and elegance, lower social class women look for bargains. African Americans react more favourably to advertisements, and buy more status products than white Americans.

But working women and men find shopping less enjoyable, and a hassle. When Americans were asked to rank their preferred activities, grocery shopping ranked 2nd from last, and other shopping came 17th (5th from last). This may have something to do with choice, most of their shopping is on essentials and hence confers no choice or control. So if we change work or work less, shopping may become more pleasurable – but it's unlikely to give long lasting happiness.

Choice

Sometimes being given lots of choice (which we might think would increase our personal control) has the opposite effect and leaves people confused and less likely to actually take decisions. Studies which presented people with 2 or 3 choices lead to more buying than when 24 choices were presented. This may be because of the perception that by choosing one, we are 'missing' 23, and since we don't have the time or the skill to tell which is best, our sense of personal control is lowered because our lack of skill or time is made especially prominent, and we react by buying nothing. Our personal control and happiness is actually reduced by too much choice. So when deciding what to do, too many choices is actually worse than just a few. New graduates often complain that there are too many careers to choose from, and frequently delay decisions for just this reason. People who have retired may find it difficult to choose what to do, because there are so many choices, rather than too few.

Low cost low choice supermarkets like Aldi and Lidl understand this, and present just one or two products in each range at low prices and are gaining customers.

Choosing a new career or job, or deciding to leave work or work part time is a major exercise in personal control, so it may feel liberating, and we may be tempted to 'just do it', particularly if our current work gives us little sense of being in control. But as we have seen, we often have misleading ideas of personal control, and we may find ourselves in a worse situation than before. So it makes sense to first look at our current role, and what affects our happiness at work. This is the focus of the next Chapter.

Andy in Bahamas (Intrepid anchored out of picture)
2015

5. Work and Job Satisfaction

> In Samoa, Eco explained that no other local family can afford the outboard motor needed to fish, and they are not able to trust each other enough to share one because some would laze around while others worked.

The earliest economists including Adam Smith regarded work as a negative, something people would only do if they had to. But there is much more to it than that. In many cases work is the central part of people's lives and can frequently be preferred to leisure. Work also usually provides our income. So how we think about work is crucial to our happiness and well-being, and any decisions about whether to change need full knowledge about this.

Work may include not for profit, which amounts to about 7% of employment in the USA (4% in UK), and other forms of care which may well not be paid (home cooking, caring, cleaning etc). 'Housework' has been measured at about 6-7 hours/day for women not in paid work, varying only a little between 1940 and the present day with seemingly no reduction due to labour saving devices, although what reduction there is seems to go to TV. Women who work full time spend about 3 hours/day on housework, those in part time work about 5 hours/day although these are broad averages. But what determines how happy we are at work?

How we feel about our work is a combination of our own personality, (eg extrovert), the job itself, (eg opportunity for personal control) and more general features like the environment we work in.

Older people in general are more satisfied with their job, about 9 out of a 10-point scale for men aged 60-64 in the USA. This compares with 7/10 for men up to age 34. Very young workers report greater job satisfaction than workers in their late twenties. For women aged above 34, job satisfaction is about 8/10 (7/10 before 34). This increase in job satisfaction with age may be due to a number of different factors including greater personal control, status etc.

Women in the USA are in general as satisfied at work as men, but women in the UK are more satisfied at work than men, although obviously individuals will differ, and the reasons for this difference are unclear. There is only a medium relationship between satisfaction in our job, and likelihood of leaving it (turnover). Greater job satisfaction does seem to go with better job performance (also a medium effect), lower absenteeism, and more discretionary or 'voluntary' activities.

Cause probably works both ways in much of this, eg high job satisfaction causes higher performance and higher performance causes greater job satisfaction – which is why even small changes to increase job satisfaction can sometimes unleash a positively reinforcing upward spiral (or vice versa). This probably justifies many of the small changes beloved by consultants and managers – sometimes even a small change can make a big difference. This effect is greater for people who are more involved in their work.

Many of us feel that work is central to our life, that it 'defines who we are' and that if we reduce our hours of work or lose status or stop altogether we will feel lost and without a purpose. This may well be the case until we work out our own sense of purpose in life, rather than letting work define it for us. However, others of us feel work is unimportant, and it seems to makes little difference to how happy we are in life – similar proportions of these two groups are very happy or fairly happy:

Satisfaction with life generally compared to how important work is considered in our life. Percentages are for UK 1999, figures in brackets are for India 2001 for comparison.

Satisfaction life generally	Work very important	Work rather important	Work not very important	Not at all important
9,10	29% (11%)	31% (2%)	24% (5%)	30% (13%)
7,8	45% (19%)	48% (19%)	44% (14%)	38% (7%)
5,6	18% (43%)	17% (43%)	21% (48%)	21% (50%)
3,4	5% (22%)	3% (28%)	9% (31%)	5% (17%)
1,2	3% (5%)	2% (10%)	1% (2%)	5% (13%)
Overall	42% (78%)	37% (18%)	10% (3%)	11% (1%)

From World Values Survey. Satisfaction with life generally is rated from 10=Satisfied to 1=Dissatisfied. Columns sum to 100% allowing for rounding.

The number in the lowest row is the % indicating how important work is to them irrespective of their happiness so 11% of British workers indicated that work is not at all important to them, as compared to 1% for India.

The difference between India and UK is marked – 78% in India regard work as very important (42% for UK), yet only 30% of these Indians are satisfied with life generally compared with 74% of the Britons. This may be changing as pay in India increases.

Greater happiness with life as a whole does seem to cause greater job satisfaction, while job satisfaction seems to cause happiness but to a lesser extent. So happy people generally make satisfied, effective employees, and satisfaction at work may cause us to come home cheerful, and thereby influence the mood of everyone. And unfortunately vice versa.

There has been a significant decrease in job satisfaction compared to leisure. In 1955 and again in 1991 American workers were asked whether they preferred work or leisure:

% saying they preferred:

	1955	1991
Working	38%	18%
Leisure	49%	68%
No Opinion	13%	14%

Satisfaction with leisure hardly changed over this period, so it seems that job satisfaction has decreased significantly in America even while household income has increased in real terms. The preference for work may reflect the idea of 'flow' championed by Csikszentmihalyi ie immersing ourself so much in an activity that we lose all sense of time, which seems to result in high levels of happiness. For some people it may be easier to do this at work than at leisure.

Some 'leisure' may even be similar to work – perhaps caring for someone or doing 'favours' for a friend or relative in exchange for similar 'favours' in return. Being able to do this confers status, and 'guanxi' in China, where much trade is based on reciprocal favours. This sort of 'leisure' is massive – some estimates are that household labour (housework caring etc) amounts to about 30% of national output.

Whether we choose to compete or co-operate at work will influence happiness Competing may yield higher income (not necessarily in the long term) but cooperating at work yields more work friends, may spill over into more general happiness, and may even yield higher income!

Our values affect our work in other ways. Unfortunately, many occupations in which less materialistic people are best suited (teaching, nursing, academia etc) often have more people wanting to do them than there are jobs, so salaries are often low.

Strong materialistic values (eg 'I admire people with expensive homes, cars and clothes') do not predict a high income, (the correlation is about zero), let alone happiness (this correlation is negative). This is bad enough, but it may be worse. Even those with the strongest materialistic values feel a need for companionship. It is just that this need is suppressed by the desire for material goods or wealth. However, since materialism leads to more unhappiness than happiness, and unhappiness leads to withdrawal from people, so their suppressed need for companionship is not met either, and the end result is likely to be unhappiness and loneliness

The individual with strong material values may perceive the 'cure' to this is to work even harder – which is unlikely to lead to any more money and is likely to result in even greater isolation. The only real solution is likely to be a more balanced approach to priorities where roughly equal value is placed on material things and friends, rather than an all or none approach, where the top value drives out all the others.

Peter Warr who is a leading work psychologist has identified 10 characteristics of jobs that will have a significant effect on happiness at work (or as it is more often known in a work context, job satisfaction). The more of each of these, the happier the worker will be, except for dimension 3:

1. Opportunity for personal control eg autonomy discretion, absence of close supervision,
2. Opportunity for skill use eg using skills we value.
3. Externally generated goals eg goals set by external factors rather than arbitrary targets. Too little of this is likely to reduce satisfaction, as is too much. 'Just the right amount' is the best level for satisfaction

4. Variety (variation in the work)
5. Clarity eg clear feedback, clear future plans, lack of insecurity, low role ambiguity.
6. Availability of money eg financial resources, pay.
7. Physical security eg absence of danger, good working conditions.
8. Supportive supervision eg support when needed, consideration, effective leadership.
9. Opportunity for interpersonal contact eg relationships with others and good opportunity to talk with them.
10. Valued social position eg feeling good about how the job is valued by ourselves and society or at least by other people we know.

In general, these effects add to each other but only up to a certain point, beyond which increases reduce job satisfaction. In particular, jobs with high demands but low opportunity for personal control can be very harmful for happiness and satisfaction and indeed for health (as they will lead to higher rates of depression and anxiety and burn out).

Of course, how we view our job – our 'model of the world' will play an important part in this, as well as the 'real' situation in the job. For example, if we view ourselves as able to influence events in our job, we are more likely to be satisfied and happier than if we feel we are powerless and have no influence. Another example of different 'mental models' may be between the employer who looks at jobs in terms of cost, productivity and output, compared to an employee who looks at pay, learning and satisfaction.

We can rate our present job, on these 10 dimensions, and on the causes of happiness already identified, and compare this with what will happen if we change jobs, downsize or stop work. The 10 factors can act as a check list to compare present and future, perhaps rating each from just right (5) to completely unacceptable (1) for each of these dimensions. But our Personality is also crucial in determining what sort of work is best for us, and how happy we will be.

Andy and Nicky on Intrepid Caribbean
2016

6. PERSONALITY, OUR VALUES AND HOW WE TAKE THE BIG DECISIONS IN OUR LIFE

> This same husband has 3 times run amok with a machete after drinking bouts – the last time Candida calmly disarmed him as he was waving the 2-foot-long cutter around. The islanders have a reputation for alcohol related violence, often in the family, but to strangers as well – underneath this well-ordered very friendly traditional matai society there are fragile personalities.

We can't change our Personality can we? Well, yes to some extent we can, and we can certainly change our habits of thinking. We can also change our values (although not very easily). However it is certainly true that Personality is one of the more stable ways of describing people. If it wasn't it would not be so useful. There are almost as many ways of describing Personality as there are Psychologists, but there have been efforts to simplify these, and some of these seem to predict happiness or contentment very well.

These dimensions are usually called the Big 2 or 3 or the Big 5 dimensions of Personality. The Big 2 are Extraversion/Introversion, and Neurotic/Stable. A Psychotic dimension is sometimes added to make this a Big 3.

The Neurotic/Stable dimension is the way we experience negative emotions or events. Individuals high on Neuroticism are typically anxious, fearful, depressed, emotional and having low self-esteem, and generally responding quickly to negative events. Alcohol seems to act by reducing inhibition, and this may be why alcohol in moderate amounts generally makes some people happier – it may well be that alcohol is reducing the effect of the neurotic/anxiety mechanism, (moving them away from the neurotic end of the scale), and therefore making these people happier temporarily. People at the Stable end of the dimension are much less reactive to mishaps and are less anxious.

Individuals high on the Extraversion dimension are characterized by being quick to respond to positive possibilities in the world, so they are sociable, assertive lively and sensation seeking, and in general the Extraversion scale seems to relate to how we react to positive emotions or events. Introverts at the opposite end of this dimension are inward looking, and often shy. People high on the Psychotic dimension are aggressive, ego-centric antisocial and creative.

So in other words, people high on the Neurotic personality dimension tend to be more aware of events which may make them unhappy; and people high on the Extraversion dimension seem to be strongly influenced and actively seek out events that may make them happy.

On the evidence from brain scans, and other sources, there does seem to be two different mechanisms, one for happiness and one for unhappiness and each is strongly genetically determined, so our baseline on each is largely determined by different genes. The personality dimensions of Neurotic and Extravert are more or less independent. In other words, we can be neurotic and extravert, or stable and extravert, or any other combination.

Evolutionary psychologists have speculated that the Neurotic and Extraversion tendencies have had evolutionary advantages like responding quickly to dangers, (Neuroticism) and cooperating, being social and seeking out food and sex (Extraversion). So it's not surprising that it appears that people don't change much on the Big 2 or 3 dimensions over time, and to a significant extent they are hereditary ie are the product of the genes we inherited from our parents. Personality measures are generally valid for at least 5 years precisely because our personality does not change much.

This may have its roots in evolution. After all, it is survival of the fittest, not of the happiest. Fortunately, nature seems to have also arranged for the happier, more open to positive opportunities to also reproduce better (even after being rebuffed dozens of times). The 2 strategies in nature ('be very alert to dangers' and 'seize all opportunities') seem to both work. Which may be why the Big 2 Personality dimensions have evolved.

The major way in which Personality can change is through traumatic events – events that are so awful that they may leave us mentally scarred for life. Those who fortunately have not had such events may find it difficult to believe but when these events occur, they can change personality and status and physiologists have even found the hormone (serotonin) that is probably causing this. What is interesting in this is that we are seeing the effect of experience overtaking genetic predisposition. So we are not completely programmed.

The other personality dimensions of the 'Big 5' have less effect on happiness or contentment. Agreeableness and Conscientiousness, seem to have a slight positive influence on happiness, and to make us slightly less unhappy; Openness to Experience (the 5th of the Big 5) seems to both increase happiness and unhappiness, but generally seems to increase happiness through adaptation – finding new ways to cope. There are many other personality scales, like the Myers Briggs, Firo-B, OPQ and so on, each of which may be mapped onto the dimensions of the Big 2, 3 or 5, and are more or less stable over time.

This strong inherited personality may appear to be bad news if we are hoping to make ourselves happy or at least contented by making changes to our life. After all if happiness is largely determined by our Personality and our Personality is more or less fixed by our genes then how can we change?

Well, firstly, even the Neurotic/Stable dimension which is about the most powerful predictor of Happiness only explains about 17% of the variance – so there is still a lot of variance; and secondly, like most hereditary influences, although some parts are fixed (so each individual has a sort of base level or natural level of happiness which we tend to revert to), we can influence this by the way we respond to the events that happen to us ie the way we react to the world and explain it to ourselves.

For example, extraverts don't just react more quickly to positive emotions and events in the world, they actually experience more positive events in total than introverts. And people high on the neurotic personality scale not only remember having more bad or negative experiences (like major arguments etc which could be due to selective memory) but also actually experience more unambiguously bad events (like divorce, break ups, bad financial affairs etc). These may be examples of 'You make your own luck'.

The second approach is to change the way we remember or think about events. So for example if an introvert compares themselves with extraverts, they may conclude that they are indeed less sociable, and 'attractive'. However, if they compare themselves to other introverts, then they may well conclude that they are actually pretty sociable, and feel good, contented and indeed happy about this. So in part it is a matter of who we compare ourselves with.

When we come to make big decisions about the future, and we use our memory of past events and our present mood, those same 'defence mechanisms' that serve us so well in keeping us relatively happy and contented (by focusing on the positives, and comparing ourselves with people who make us, by comparison, feel pretty good) may seriously mislead us. For example, the mild introvert who is in a team of strong introverts and computer nerds, may be the life and soul of the party at work but when they apply for a job in selling may well find that they are almost literally in a different league.

The third way we can try to change our Personality is to change our values. This may occur through a religious or spiritual change; or a life change experience such as a near miss or more prosaically a self-help class or book; or it may be a conscious re-evaluation of what is important to us, and what we genuinely feel threatens us and our sense of self esteem. So for example after a heart attack we may decide that material goods don't really matter very much at all, whereas family and friends do. This changed set of values is likely to affect the way we behave – in effect our personality - and indeed our ability to be happy. A highly materialistic set of values (focusing on high status goods and possessions and positions) seems to be correlated with significantly less happiness, and as we shall see, these values are often passed onto us from our parents, and we pass them on to our children.

When pay is totally determined by results, people learn a very focused form of behaviour – they only work for what they are paid for and ignore everything else. This can change our values (work ethic, materialistic values etc) as well as our day to day behaviour. So how we are paid can distort our values. This is explored in Appendix 1.

A related set of values arises from the search for perfection. Although admirable in some circumstances, it seems that 'satisficers' (ie those people who look for something that fits the functionality required), are more likely to be happy than 'maximisers' (ie people who seek perfection even when this level of functionality is not required). This requires us to decide when perfection is needed and when it is not, and getting a coherent set of values about this is likely to have a significant effect on our happiness.

Up to now we have largely focused on work. But even if we are focusing on our work and when and how to change jobs, or stop altogether, we will still be influenced by our life outside work, so we need to explore how our private life can affect our happiness, and how this interacts with work.

Sunset from Intrepid, USA
2015

7. Marriage, Cohabiting, Sex, Divorce, Separation and Children

> Peter and Sarah finally met, and it was love at first sight. Obviously the air in the Pacific makes things just... happen... they think the world of each other, and within an hour or so Sarah had postponed her flight to be with him, and I made a mental note to check that Sarah had not stowed away when we left Galapagos. Peter tells us every hour that she is a wonderful girl... (we just agree)

We may think that money is the route to happiness but as we have seen we would usually be wrong. So perhaps happiness is marriage and children? Well, studies do seem to indicate that marriage slightly increases happiness (by about 4% over being single) and divorce reduces happiness (by about 5%) although these are broad averages. Separating reduces happiness even more (by about 8%). Cohabiting gives less of an increase in happiness than marriage. So whilst not a sure fire guarantee of happiness, marriage does seem to make people happier on average. Of course knowing this and putting it into practice are two very different things, but we may at least know the figures.

Now a 4% increase in happiness may not seem like very much, and indeed it's not (even allowing for the inevitable generalizing about such a specific figure). There are a number of other factors which have a much bigger effect, and they are covered elsewhere. However this perhaps illustrates better than anything else that whilst figures such as this may look useful in our pursuit of happiness, in fact it is more difficult for us as individuals to know what to do with them. Suppose that we are single and want to be happier. Does it mean that we should rush out and marry quickly? Clearly not, yet many people may do just this, especially if their attention is continually drawn to 'biological clocks' or 'being left on the shelf' or even 'celebrity marriages'. The issue is clearly a more complex one: what distinguishes a marriage in which both partners are happier than they were before (or to be even more complicated, than they would have been if they were not married?).

Let's dig a bit deeper:

	Very Happy Men	Very Happy Women	Depressed (Men and Women)
Married	38%	42%	1.5%
Single, Never Married	21%	26%	2.3%
Separated	18%	21%	
Divorced	16%	17%	Divorced once 4%; Twice 6 %
Cohabiting	n/a	n/a	5%

(ie 38% of married men rated themselves as very happy, whereas only 18% of men who are separated rated themselves as very happy; 26% of single, never married women rated themselves as very happy etc).

Marriage

Why are married men and women happier and less likely to be depressed? Is it because married people are on average older? And why are cohabiting couples twice as likely to be depressed as singles? What is the cause? This will be different for each individual circumstance, but it probably includes:

1. Perspective – married people have more formal roles and perspectives to see themselves in – if they are doing badly at work for example, they may at least comfort themselves that they are a good husband or wife.
2. The intimacy, friendship and openness which are characteristic of a good marriage are likely to lead to increased happiness (although clearly this could also be the case in cohabiting couples).
3. There may be a greater sense of security – or at least less anxiety – because there is a degree of mutual commitment to support each other and stay together even when times are hard, which is not present (at least in a formal sense) with cohabiting couples.

The way we regard relationships varies between cultures – in the west it is more likely to involve individualism, and self-expression, whereas Asian and 3rd world cultures are more likely to be collectivist, placing greater value on duty and the welfare of the group. People from collectivist cultures tend to have fewer relationships, but they are deeper and longer lasting. There even seems to be a difference between how people 'feel good'. In the west this often seems to be individualistic, eg feeling proud, whereas in collectivist cultures, it more often means having friendly feelings or mutual loyalty or being interdependent.

Unfortunately, in spite of the plethora of dating and introduction agencies many of which claim to be able to pair us up with 'our ideal partner', there is no clear or widely accepted rule for what does distinguish a marriage that makes both partners happier, although there are some indications that far from 'opposites attracting', it may make for a happier relationship if both partners are similar in personality and interests, (although not identical). However this will in any case vary over time, (marriages seem to be happiest at the start and when any children have left home, with quite a pronounced dip in between – on average), and it may be that we can take romantic engineering too far.

But the relatively small effect of 'married/not married' on happiness, means that if we are single we should not rush out and try to marry anyone – if we never get married we are still likely to be happier (and less depressed) than a significant proportion of married or cohabiting people. Happiness levels seem to be pretty much the same for marrieds, singles, and widowed; people who are divorced are overall unhappier, but of course this will depend on individual circumstances, and the individuals may well be happier than when they were married.

Satisfied with life in general UK 1999 World Values Survey

Satisfaction	Married	Divorced	Widowed	Single, Never Married
9,10	32%	19%	32%	30%
7,8	46%	45%	33%	43%
5,6	16%	22%	25%	18%
3,4	4%	6%	11%	6%
1,2	1%	8%	1%	3%

The question asked was 'All things considered, how satisfied are you with your life as a whole these days? 1 Dissatisfied 10 Satisfied.

The relationship between a happy marriage and individual happiness is high, although we cannot necessarily say that one causes the other. So a happy marriage is worth waiting for, a marriage at any cost is not.

To what extent is getting married actually within our control? Given the many personal ads and dating agencies, many single people want to get into a relationship, but are not. This has some parallels with getting a job – we may all want a wonderful job – but getting it may prove much more difficult. I have tried using head-hunting approaches to find a partner for some people – the parallels work fairly well.

The process of clarifying criteria, examining our sources of knowledge for who meets these (long list) then narrowing this down by personal contact, and finally the almost ritualized mating game (in both work and romance) of exploratory initial moves which have a low risk of embarrassment ('let's meet for a drink') through to more serious exploration on what could be the basis for a long lasting relationship. And of course marriage (and employment) are specific and formalized types of relationship – there are others.

Sex

Sex is one of the most happiness inducing activities – at least according to a survey of American ladies. In this survey sex rated at the top of preferred activities in a typical week. And marriage or cohabitation gives more opportunities for sex (usually that is) so this may be a further reason for marriage and living together making people happy. People cohabiting report having more sex (on average) than married couples, which may reflect more fun or fewer children or novelty or even a desire to retain commitment in the absence of formal ties.

Attractive women have better sex lives and more faithful lovers, while preferred mates are generally high status or reliable earners. So in the case of marriage or cohabitation, there is also a type of reference group, in which happiness is believing that compared to our reference group we are getting a 'good deal' in the short and long term taking account of the potential of the other for further development. Recent research has indicated that when there is a scarcity of women, they choose men of high status to marry eg when there were 110 males to 100 females (Arizona 1910) only 24% low status men were married at age 30, compared to 46% high status men. From an evolutionary standpoint women were probably looking for a good provider, and given the relative scarcity of women, could get a good deal. If each partner believes this, then the partnership is likely to survive, but the real test will be when (at some time – there always will be) one believes that they have given more than they are receiving.

If our aspirations for a high status partner are increased by advertising and celebrity worship or even Playboy or Cosmopolitan, then we are less likely to find someone who we regard as a good deal. The search for the perfect drives the good out of contention, just as the focus on the short term may divert us from the long term relationship. Articles in Cosmopolitan have changed from the 1960's when 90% focused on marriage and children, (in a positive or neutral way), to the 2000's when most articles concentrate on short term dating, only 5% of articles on men focus on marriage and 2/3 of the articles on marriage are negative or neutral towards it.

Most divorces are initiated by women, and 15 years after, a majority feels that divorce has been good for them (although it may not be good for children as we shall see). Books like 'The Rules' (written by women) which terrifyingly describes the ways that dating 'should' proceed in New York, try to redress the supply demand imbalance inherent in greater female sexual freedom elsewhere.

Midlife

For both women and men, midlife often brings sexual problems (menopause and the male menopause which can be anything from 38-55). Gail Sheahy and Leone Sugarman describe these very well. Men and women who have always regarded their attractiveness and sexual potency as key to their character have to come to terms with what they may easily regard as failure – finding it harder to compete with younger people. For men this may be made worse by the realisation that in very many cases the woman is earning as much or more than the man. In the USA in 55% of households, the woman is earning at least half of the household income.

The search for happiness in marriage or cohabitation requires relationship management. Frequently angst at life in general is taken out on our partner or close friend. A common tactic is trying to arrange consequences to 'teach the other a lesson'. 'I'll show him what it's like if I don't clean the kitchen' can become a tit for tat of 'I'll show her what it's like if I don't mend the plumbing'. Or even as Eric Berne described in Games People Play, Adult/Child 'I am forbidding you to do that' or Child/Adult 'I can't do anything for myself'. The only way around this is communication, describing the problem in a low key unaroused way looking for a joint problem solving approach and resisting the temptation to raise the temperature. Some people make it a rule never to discuss these issues after alcohol.

Books like Men are from Mars, Women are from Venus explain why men and women's attempts to help each other sometimes back-fire. So for example when a man has a problem, he will expect practical solutions, and if all he gets is emotional support, ('I still love you') this may be seen as deliberately unhelpful; whereas when the woman has a problem, she expects emotional support ('I still love you') and when all she gets is practical solutions ('Call a plumber') regards this as being callous and unfeeling.

Roles will change from individual to partner, to parent, to carer. This may involve redefining goals, deciding what we really want to do – which may or may not mean staying in the marriage.

The role of Government

If we look at the situation from the point of view of 'Society' or the Government rather than an individual, we may focus on different aspects and come to different conclusions. The reason why these conclusions may be different is that Governments tend to regard themselves as responsible for creating and defending the conditions which enable individual citizens to live, work, create wealth and ... pursue happiness. We will talk later about whether Governments should more explicitly target an increase in national happiness as a goal (if it is, they do not seem to be doing a very good job of it), but if marriage does cause happier citizens, then it would seem reasonable for the government to encourage it.

Up to now we have focused mainly on the happiness caused by differences between individuals. But there are some effects that can be significantly influenced by governments and it may be as well to investigate the case of marriage and cohabitation because it nicely illustrates this.

It could be argued that if marriage makes people happier, then there is no need for Government to do anything more. But as we have seen we are very easily swayed by everything from advertisements to celebrities, and even by laws and government inducements. So although we may want to have another drink before we drive home, we may be deterred by our memory of the explicit drink drive advert showing graphic footage of a road accident, and if not by that, then by the deterrent of being banned from driving, fined and perhaps imprisoned. So Governments sometimes have to influence or coerce us to do what we may not always do left to ourselves. Education, Nudges, Inducement and Compulsion are the means by which Governments try to control the behaviour of their citizens.

And we do know that in Britain at least, marriage is becoming less and less common, at the same time that Britons are no happier than they were 30 years ago in spite of massive extra real income; and Britain's children are rated as some of the least happy in Europe. So if government knows that marriage makes people on average happier, and yet marriage is reducing in frequency significantly, then there is a good case for Governments to examine why, and whether there is anything they can do about it.

Higher income earners seem to be more likely to marry and make commitments. This may be caused by the high income, or by other factors which affect both income and likelihood to marry, for example the values passed down from parents emphasizing the value of discipline, commitment, prudence, and delaying gratification. Higher education seems to persuade women (but not men) to have fewer children. At age 42, 1/3 of women with a higher degree are childless, compared to 20% for those with A levels or better, and 10% of those with no or few school leaving qualifications. Once women have decided to have children, family size seems to be about the same for all levels of education.

Divorce and Separation

But there may be more to it than that – studies have shown that children of parents who are divorced or separated are more likely to have materialistic values, have twice the probability of being depressed, or being suspended from school, and seven times the chance of being imprisoned, and on average will live 4 years less. And in USA's major cities, over half of the children are being brought up in one parent families or whose parents are not married (which is not the same thing but may be related). The figures for UK are close behind, and we have seen that British children are some of the unhappiest in Europe. This affects us all either directly or indirectly.

Even death of a parent can lead to unhappiness. There is evidence that the death of a parent during childhood (up to age 11) is directly linked to alcoholism in daughters, even allowing for any possible genetic pre-disposition. (Which is not of course to say this necessarily happens).

These are hard hitting figures which have implications almost everywhere, from schools to crime, from housing to health to wealth. So there is a serious issue to do with keeping parents together, and marriage may well be a strong influence in this respect. If we found that being married keeps parents together longer and better than if they just cohabit, and it is better for children, then it would seem reasonable and fair to encourage parents to marry. We could even argue that in an evolutionary sense the long term pairing of parents (of many species) seems to confer benefits.

We could also think about the long term costs of care in old age or following illness or accident. Studies have demonstrated that long term couples usually learn to divide tasks up very effectively so that they are more efficient than independent pairs of individuals. Married couples communicate better and develop mutually complementary skills. These benefits of being together probably originate in evolution (although part learned) and are crucial in helping couples stay together during the times when a relationship is under strain. On Intrepid, Nicky tends to do the navigation; I tend to do the maintenance. We are each more efficient for being able to specialize in this way. Consultants and Economists have for years extolled the virtues of specialization, and the law of comparative advantage (which in brief means it is better to do what you are best at, than to try to do everything). The benefits come from greater close quarters experience, and close cohabiting or marriage gives exactly these benefits. Why not take advantage of them? After all we would not normally try to build our own car or dishwasher by ourselves?

Growing Old

Do you want to grow old together or grow old alone? Longer term a couple can provide care and support for each other in a much more effective way than the 4 or 5 professional carers that might be needed to provide 24-hour care, possibly funded or subsidized by the Government, plus if we avoid more single person households, we reduce the need for much new housing. The Government would be using enlightened self-interest to persuade us to 'buddy up' even if we ignore romance, just as armed forces find that casualty rates reduce significantly if soldiers team up and care for their buddy.

At the moment it comes 'for free' in the form of unpaid carers who would cost in the UK about 40 billion pounds in 1992 money, or 7% of GNP. 83% of this was caring for people aged 65 and over. Put this way, a commitment to care for any children we have and to care for the other in 'sickness and in health' would seem to be a reasonable contribution to justify some encouragement from the government in some form of 'civil contract' (If Government provide some extra support, will you commit to care for each other in sickness and old age and raise the children you have?). Or to reverse the causation, the Government would do well to explicitly encourage people to marry when there are children and/or when long or short term care for one or another partner is likely to be needed. (Note all this can apply equally to different and same sex marriages when it comes to mutual care, and even in cases where a same sex couple are caring for children). The problem is that as we have seen, when money is put into the equation, unpaid work tends to stop very quickly unless it is paid for.

If Government were to decide to encourage marriage especially when there are children, how could it do so most effectively? The first point would be to avoid as far as possible any stigma or inequality on children whose parents are not married – it would be absurd to try to create a better situation for children and end up favouring one group (children of married parents) over the other. So the mechanism should not be applied at the level of the child, but rather at the adults. One mechanism could be via pension (ie when children have left home). At the moment the pension for married couples may be less than two singles. If this were improved to bring it into line with two singles, there would be more of an incentive to marry and care for each other. More immediately there could be income tax benefits to recognise the long term care commitments made, a bit like tax benefits to encourage people to save for their old age.

Children

Well, if marriage makes us happier does having children? On the evidence, this is questionable. Children make us happy when they are born, but the effect wears off quickly. Couples are happier before the first child is born than after. This may have to do with the protective bonding effect, where the woman's horizons narrow sharply, the man stops being the main focus of attention, sex may reduce in frequency, and the man may feel reduced to 'just' the breadwinner at the same time that his hours at work and his income are often increasing rapidly and his attraction to others increasing with it.

The cost of children can be staggering – one estimate is that two children in the UK would cost a couple over £200,000 in costs and lost income, and this can lead to debt or unhappiness if it drives the household income below a reasonable minimum.

About 20% of couples find it difficult to have babies for various reasons, and these difficulties get worse the later the decision to start (which increasingly is the trend). For example, marriage is coming later (27 on average in UK, 25 in USA up from 21 and 20 respectively in the 1950/60's). This makes the fact that 85% of women have a baby at some time in their life seem high all things considering, especially as even with the most enlightened workplace policies there is still an impact on work

As for looking after children, one study on working women in Texas, USA found that looking after children rated not much higher in terms of happiness than discussions with their boss! The real improvement in happiness seems to come when the children leave home, so the empty nest syndrome actually seems to go with greater happiness not less. What really made these ladies happiest was sex and talking with their friends, and certainly friends seems to be one of the major factors in whether people are happy or not. This is explored in the next Chapter.

We might think that in Asian societies which generally have had a lower rate of divorce, and stronger family ties, the picture would be different. But with increasing commercialization, even this is changing. Whereas 66% of people in China said that they would take care of parents by all means, this was only 46% in USA and just 16% in Japan. In Japan the average time a father spends with his children is just 36 minutes/day, compared to 56 minutes/day in the USA, which may be what is causing the care figures; or it may be the pronounced materialism in Japan, which is higher than USA or UK.

In the Great Depression when unemployment was up to 30%, the worst effect on children was the stress induced in their parents, far more than any shortage of food or material goods. Currently American women report a 20% reduction in time available for family care. The relatively high care figures for China (filial piety) may themselves even be changing as free market thinking there becomes more pervasive, to say nothing of the as yet unknown effect of the one child policy on subsequent parental care ('all the care on my shoulders and a drag on my career').

This has clear implications for our future. In the past people were able to 'rely' on children to look after them in old age; now, with lengthening old age, it seems much less likely that children will care for elderly parents to the same extent – and we are tending to have fewer children anyway. So as we grow older we may need to have monetary assets to buy care that in the past children used to provide. In other words using a market solution to the problem that market forces may well have aggravated in the first place by weakening family ties.

Extended Families

With increasing numbers of people having no children and no partner, it is likely that the extended family and relatives (brothers, sisters, cousins etc) are going to be asked more for care. But of course one child families will also dry up this source of emotional, financial and practical support, and there needs to be a 'feel good' factor to this caring for it to be robust enough to continue.

Extended families can have other effects. Let's start with something I noticed in a country where extended families are strong. Workers were sometimes requesting that when they were promoted, there was no announcement, so that only they knew about their promotion. At first sight this seemed strange – after all business psychologists or good CEO's know that people like to have good work recognised, to be seen to be good performers is motivating, that the positive opinion of those around us is important. So why were these people trying to hush up their promotion?

The reason, I eventually discovered is that in this country (like many others), there is a very large extended family, which is often supported by the income of only a few breadwinners. The size of this extended family, and the demands made will depend to some extent on their perceived income. So if it is known that a person has been promoted, and gained (shall we say) a large bonus or a 10% increase, then those already in the extended family will each expect more, and a few others with some claim to belong to this extended family will also claim their share. So the only effect of the promotion or bonus will be to increase the demands on the individual, and will not actually result in the worker having more money. And the effect of a bonus is 'worse' than the promotion because the bonus will increase demands in the short term but does not guarantee extra income next year – the bonus next year may be smaller or non exist-ent. It could be argued that in a wider sense the worker should not be 'selfish' but the fact remains that the only effect of the extra money from the promotion is likely to increase demands, not increase happiness.

So the effects of extended families can be complex. Extra money will be beneficial to those receiving it, and it may increase the 'status' of the person promoted not only in the organisation but also in their extended family. It may also 'bank' significant good will that may be called upon in the future.

So if we are thinking about changing jobs or leaving work altogether, there are some powerful arguments in favour of retaining our partner if we have one, and try to reinforce contacts with children and relatives. The extended family that may seem like a burden at times may be a life-line in future. This is a lot more than financial. Relationships that do not have effort put into them wither, so if we think about this carefully, we may regard an investment of effort into these relationships as enlight-ened self interest, likely to pay back at some time in the future.

But then of course there are always Friends...

Intrepid in Bahamas National Park
2016

8. Friends and Social Groups and living alone or together

> Yesterday 30 naive dolphins met us in mid Pacific. They are smaller than Atlantic ones, and they can't see many boats – they kept their distance at first but later came closer and showed off doing flips and belly flops, and stayed almost the whole night. This was our first contact with another mammal for a whole week so I am afraid we clustered around the bow trying to communicate... Pathetic isn't it?

Recall that the most favoured activity of American women (after sex) was talking to friends. Layard concluded that the most important factor determining happiness seems to be Family Relationships, and the single activity we seem to like most is talking with friends. But something is happening in America which Putnam called 'Bowling Alone' – a reduction in the number of people going out in groups, or volunteering. This is a complicated issue and trends such as a rise in gangs, and large binge drinking parties, going out to clubs, cinemas or live sports (as opposed to watching it on TV), while they may not in the longer term always make the people involved happier, are still evidence that we continue to enjoy interacting in groups, and people with more friends are happier.

As always there is the issue of what causes what? Do happy people make more friends, or do more friends make people happier? There is no especially good evidence on this, but it seems reasonable to conclude that causation is in both directions – so happy people make more friends, and having more friends makes us happy.

Indeed it may well be that having a number of different sets of friends has a more robust effect than if all our friends are from the same source, just work for example. (This is a parallel to the multiple roles in marriage providing greater resilience when things go wrong). Not only will we have 'safety in numbers' but if for whatever reason we do something to lower our sense of self esteem and/or lose one set of friends (say at work), then we have other sets of friends who are unaffected (perhaps at our local club or pub, or our relatives) who will provide support.

Depression

The greater diversity of friends may also mean that whenever we need to 'phone a friend' or 'borrow a shoulder to cry on' or just to have a good laugh or outing, we have someone with the right skills and approach. Indeed, when individuals are coping with depression or unhappiness, friends are often as effective as therapists.

Even depression can be offset by conversations with friends who offer a different perspective from the sense of self-induced failure symptomatic of depression felt by even the most successful of people, Sir Winston Churchill for example. Deep depression though will respond best to a mix of anti-depressant drugs and discussions with friends or professionals. Less helpfully, in France and the USA, the alcohol consumption of friends was a more powerful predictor of youthful drinking than any individual characteristics or parental drinking habits.

Culture

This illustrates some of the cultural issues in our enjoyment. In Asian and collectivist societies, there is a tendency to emphasise loyalty to the group, and to have fewer, longer conversations, whereas in the more western, more individualistic cultures, conversations tend to be quicker, and shallower ('Have a nice day' culture). Some people even trace this development of individualism in the West to the change from traditional agricultural life dominated by family and convention, to modern, individualistic, city, capitalist life dominated by the role of the individual and their contract with the employer. It will be interesting to see how this works out in China and India.

These two major trends – the increase in individualism; and in city dwelling affect friendships and happiness in complex ways.

Living Alone

Consider living alone versus living with others. In UK and USA there has been an increasing tendency to live alone rather than together with either a family or friends. Children, who might in the past have lived with their parents, move out to their own apartment by themselves or with friends. Parents who when they retire might have moved in with their children, now continue to live by themselves, often even after one has died. As divorce and partnership separation increase, so the splinters live separately.

In the 1990's in UK and USA about 25% of adults were living singly. About half of these had no or few ongoing sexual relations, the other half had sexual relations at about the same level as married couples! So we are increasingly living alone – which even with the sex may not be good for our happiness. We may think we would be happier living alone, perhaps because we would have more personal control over our lives – we can do whatever we want, and there is no-one to complain. But maybe that is exactly the point.

This may be an example of our thinking misleading us. If we are living with others, what will attract our attention? Probably having to share things, give up things, (not watching the TV we want, because they want something else), do tasks now when we want to do them later, (cleaning the kitchen or bathroom for example) noise, arguments etc. These factors are therefore particularly important to us, and when we compare living by ourselves and living with others, we will tend to think particularly about those factors impacting on us at the moment; and we are likely to overlook the things that may face us living alone – loneliness, extra cost, inconvenience when you go away or have things delivered, or when we are ill etc. So deciding to live alone may be a case of us paying attention to only those factors important to us at the time, and not to those that people already living by themselves consider important. 'The grass is always greener on the other side of the fence' This will be explored more in Chapter 19.

Given the increase in living alone, one might think that we would see more people visiting each other. But this has also fallen – from 30% who frequently (several times/week) spend a social evening with neighbours in 1970's to 22% in 1990's, and from 38% who frequently spend an evening with relatives in 1970's to 34% in 1990's (both these figures from the USA). The proportion of people who spend evenings with parents seems more constant at about 19%, and visiting friends also the same at about 22%.

One may argue that this is offset partially by emails, phone, messaging and social networking sites, and anyway we may be seeing the effect of frequent re-locations because of work demands which move people away from relatives. But the reduction in time spent with neighbours is not explained by this. It may however be caused by more TV watching, which also seems to lower trust, and increase a sense of being victimized. Children's TV viewing reduces playing with friends, and tends to make them identify with artificial TV heroes. We may be seeing what Robert Lane has called the 'cold society'.

One might think that the significant increase in women working would result in an increase in friends, as well as the income that the work brings. Unfortunately, it appears that there is no increase in friends outside the family at all. Presumably friends made at work are offset by a loss of friends near the home.

Moving Home

This is relevant for where we choose to live. Some of the happiest people seem to be those who have stopped work and have stayed living where they are, rather than moving, so that they are with friends whom they have known for years. That is not to say that moving house is wrong, just that we need to take a long hard look at what we will miss if we move.

Whilst over-crowding can cause unhappiness, misery and even ill-health, living alone can also cause ill health. A study of heart attack patients found that those living alone were twice as likely to have a recurrence as those who lived with someone else. Generally the survival rate for illnesses seems to be twice as high if there is significant emotional support – often provided by friends.

This is important because lonely people tend to adapt to loneliness, and when asked are not very interested in making new friends. This defence mechanism may be counter-productive, given the physical and emotional consequences of living alone.

What we look for in friends

A British study by Argyle and Furnham found that what people meant by companionship involved mainly material and practical help', perhaps more than emotional help. There may be differences between the sexes here as already mentioned in Men are from Mars, Women from Venus. Women expect and offer more emotional support, whereas men expect and want practical solutions.

Work and business has always involved ties of friendship, but in the last 50 years there have been two countervailing forces – 1. A more arm's length contractual relationship where business goes to the lower bidder perhaps on the internet, irrespective of friendship, often strictly audited to prevent favouritism, and financial or emotional bribery; and 2. Growth in networking, customer relationships, lobbying and head-hunting which relies on business relationships and connections.

We can even think of 'investing' in friendship. 57% of Britons regard friends as very important 38% as rather important, only 5% regard friends as not very important. This last group is a little unhappier than the rest but there is no difference in happiness between the first two groups.

Leaving aside the Machiavellian aspect already considered, we may decide to cultivate this or that friendship according to how much bene-fit we are likely to get in practical or emotional support when needed. Some economists and psychologists have even tried to estimate the pay-back period with predictably confusing results. Some find friend-ships take a long time to payback, others argue that we receive benefits from Day 1 of a friendship, so the payback is actually immediate. So maybe new friends are as good for us as old ones. And we learn how to make friends by practice, so this can be doubly reinforcing. Earlier communities in the West and current Asian societies still have a very strong emphasis on neighbours helping each other, and these produce real mutual benefits.

Of course, if our friends don't live with us, we can to a greater extent take them or leave them. So having friends and a convenient focal point where we all gather may well be an important factor in happiness – which may be why so many TV series revolve around a bar or pub or street corner – we need friends and a place to meet them when we want to, but not when we don't. We live 50 metres from a local pub where individuals can gather when they want to.

Trust

Then there is the issue of trust. There seems to be a small increase in our happiness if we feel we can trust those in the community in which we live. This robust effect is influenced by our own personality, by our own income, whether we live in a small rural community; or a town or city, and by events that have occurred to us. But these can also involve friends. Friends are often there when we need them for example after an accident.

Some events can be so traumatic that we never really recover from them, even if we are offered counselling. However, there is mixed evidence on whether extensive post traumatic stress counseling does any good. A self disciplined approach focusing on living a normal life and getting on with friends can be as good as or better than counseling which may resurface distressing events.

Either way, living near friends, and people and communities we feel we can trust is likely to make a small but useful increase in our happiness, and this is especially important as family relationships weaken. As we have seen, it can even make us healthier – which is another important factor in making us happy or unhappy.

Atlantic crossing completed with Beryl, Bernard, Nicky, Andy

9. Health

> Candida's father had been a bright outgoing person until the cyclone hit, and he watched all his work of the previous 20 years destroyed in one day. The event so traumatized him, that he never even started to rebuild and replant, and now 7 years later just watches TV.

Major depression (which is treated as an illness) or even minor depression makes us unhappy. However physical illness eg a 20% drop in health also reduces happiness – by about 6%. Add to this the loss of personal freedom or control that ill-health often entails – to say nothing of its effect on income, friends, our family etc.

On the other hand we seem to be able to adapt to ill health to a very significant extent – if we want to. The most extreme examples of this are paraplegics who seem to be only a few percent less happy than able bodied people – the paraplegics seem to focus on what they have rather than what they have not, and it is rather able bodied people in the presence of disabled people whose happiness seems to drop.

There is also an interaction the other way round, the happier we are the more likely we are to be healthy – partly because we exercise more, and partly because happier people have stronger immune systems. Medically, it appears that serotonin deficiency (a brain chemical which is itself partially genetically linked) is a strong indicator of anxiety and depression, so some 'cures' are related to correcting this. There is though the countervailing factor, that extraverts (who are happier in general) are more likely to have accidents.

Health tends to decrease as we get older, but we also seem to adapt to this which is why older people are marginally happier than young ones. However we have to recognise that our ability to do various things especially physical activities will reduce as we get older, and the time taken to recover from ailments gets longer. Therefore if we particularly want to do something, we should do it before we are unable to do so – otherwise we may regret having worked when we might have done something that we really wanted to do. Put this way, wealth health, time and skills are the crucial resources we need to do many of the activities which make us happy and fulfilled. Health is one that will not always be with us, (we can't store it), and so we need to make best use of it when we can.

Social Class

This Chapter is mainly concerned with the effect of health on happiness, but there is a factor common to both which has a major effect on health. People in high social class are healthier and live longer than people in the lowest social class. This may not be causative by itself, rather the result of other factors like smoking, obesity, murder, suicide, and accidents, but it is important nonetheless. Social class affects health significantly and the effect is increasing not decreasing. In the 1970's, unskilled workers could expect to live 5 years less than professionals; in the 2000's the figure is 9 years less. In the UK, in 2000's men in routine jobs are 2.8 times more likely to die between the ages of 25 and 64 years than men in higher managerial posts. In 1991 the risk factor was 2.9 times.

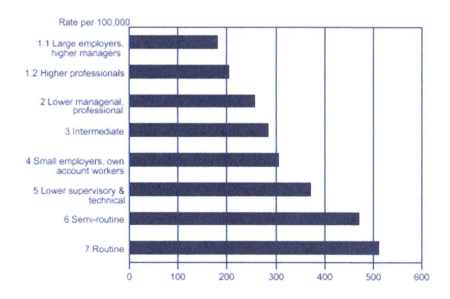

Age-standardised deaths/100,000 workers by Socio Economic Class: men aged 25-64, England and Wales 2001-03

There is also a race difference. In the USA a teenager has a 75% chance of reaching 65; but if they are black, the chances are just 25%.

Loss of income also has a significant adverse effect on health – much more than an increase in income improves health. Richer people are both fitter and healthier – partly because of better medical attention, but also because of greater encouragement to eat sensibly and exercise frequently. But clearly this is something that is in our own hands – it's no use complaining that we don't have enough money for a personal trainer, when the best personal trainer may well be ourself – or a team of our friends who all train together.

Our attitude to ill health

But the main determinant of whether ill health makes us unhappier is probably our own attitude to it. If we can't change it, then we may as well focus on what we can do with what we have, rather than focus on what we can no longer do. This is exactly what a business should do if it loses a competitive advantage (like patents expiring for a drug firm), and people are no different.

There is some inspiring work by top class sportsmen who have had to recover from near death crippling accidents (eg a car smash). The contrast between what these sportsmen were able to do before and after the accident could not have been more extreme, going from world class athletic prowess to someone who could not even walk.

They developed an integrated 6 stage approach to recovery based on Neuro Linguistic Programming (NLP) principles which relies on a positive mental attitude, and which has been demonstrated to work:

1. Commit to a particular inspiring goal, or to eliminate a difficulty.
2. Set high standards
3. Take it one step at a time – identify a measurable improvement that can be accomplished each day however small.
4. Manage your perception of time. For these small steps focus on the present. Don't get distracted by maybe's or future problems. But also visualise the positive image of what you will become.
5. Be part of the rehabilitation – get involved, don't let the medical staff treat you as a passive object. Be active, don't be objectionable

but understand what is being done and help with it.

6. Don't compare yourself with others; this will only make you miserable. Instead compare yourself with how you were one week ago, or whatever time frame is best.

The 6 points are not stages in recovery so much as a complete 6 point plan, each is important This approach was developed by a sportsman who was very badly injured. He was also an NLP practitioner, and although he could easily have given up altogether given the enormity of his injuries, he used these principles to help his recovery, and subsequently uses it to help others. This is a very good example of how our perception of ourselves and our situation can make a massive difference to our well-being and our health.

Point 5 (active mentality) is critical and was tested in a nursing home where half the people were given instructions on their responsibility for themselves, while the remainder were told how important it was for the staff to take good care of them. The active (first) group showed better well-being, were happier and even lived years longer than the passive (second) group.

Friends

The other major factor affecting our recovery from ill health is our friends. As we have seen in the last chapter, there is good evidence that having at least one confidant or close friend makes a significant difference not just to the well being and happiness of the person who is ill, but also significantly improves their rate of recovery and reduces their chances of early death even from illnesses as severe and as apparently independent of positive thinking as cancer and heart disease. By contrast living alone may make it more difficult to recover from illness, let alone the practical difficulties.

We also need to consider the effect of spiritual values and religion. This is covered next.

Sailing to the finish, end of 2nd Atlantic crossing

10. Religion

Apart from volcanic eruptions, the main events in Samoa are cyclones – 2 massive ones hit in 1990 and 1991, deforesting much of the island with 6 metre waves, 180 mph winds, and salt that coated trees and killed them because the cyclone takes all the moisture from surrounding air, and it didn't rain for the next 2 months. So the first response of the community leaders was to ... rebuild the damaged churches. For example 3 million Talla for one Congregational Church, the community is still paying off the debt. Funny priorities to have 200 churches for 40,000 people, and 2 doctors. But to Samoans (and to English people for 100's of years – think of all the churches in England) it makes sense – religion has always been central to their community. Indeed in Samoa we went to the largest step pyramid in the Pacific, Pulemetai, 65 metres x 60 square at the top, about 100 metres x 100 at the pae pae (lower platform) level, 14 metres high, with a sunken entrance stairway, all hand built of lava rock, probably when the Tongans occupied Samoa in about 1200 – 1500AD. 30,000 cubic metres of rock, I guess church building came naturally to them when the missionaries first came ashore in 1830.

The effect of religion on happiness seems to be robust but relatively small – about 2-3% of the variation in happiness can be explained by religion. There does not seem to be good evidence on whether any particular religion is better than any other at making its believers happier – at least in this world – but they may well argue that this is not the main purpose of religion. It may even be that this small increase in happiness shown by those who belong to a religion may be due to the many social benefits gained by religious events, mutual support etc.

> 'One of the few mechanisms for regular interaction in the suburbs is the church. Many people attend church for social reasons initially, not to satisfy a spiritual need'. Letter to the Economist 1ˢᵗ December 2007

It may however be due to an inherently 'better' sense of values – people whose values place greater importance on having close friends and family and marriage and self-discipline rather than an important high status position and all the trappings of power do seem to be happier, and many religions may well claim that the former set of values (close friends etc) is close to the values espoused by their religion.

Of course this does not mean that all atheists are unhappy – indeed if this causation is correct, then atheists with many friends and a set of values that places high value on self discipline friends etc may well be very happy, whereas someone with religion who values positions of status and power may well be very unhappy.

Nevertheless, there does seem to be something positively enjoyable in praying, worshipping or meditating. In the survey of American women mentioned earlier, praying worshipping or meditating rated high in enjoyment, (about the same as eating and exercise), and the emphasis on the spiritual can be an important counter balance to the uncertain stressful material world.

Countries and communities vary in how much emphasis they place on religion as opposed to for example rational, secular thought. More 'traditional' communities may have religion as a central focus in their lives, (this is not to say it makes them any happier or unhappier, just that it figures prominently). In the USA of course, rational thought and religious values are both given prominence, which is why issues such as evolution/intelligent design and pro-choice/right to life are hotly debated.

The strong emphasis placed by many religions on blind faith can be seen as an example of 'cognitive dissonance'. This is explored in a later Chapter, but in brief, suppose we choose to join a religious group, and the consequence is that we experience significant persecution or cost.

The logical response if we are to remain in the religion is to affirm that the ultimate rewards are far greater than the costs, and the probability of gaining these rewards is very high or even absolutely certain. To do anything else is to question our logic, and to place significant stress on ourselves by having inconsistent ideas. (If the reward is only moderate, and the probability of getting it only medium while the costs are so high, then why am I persisting in being a member of this religion?)

So it is no surprise that many religions increase the rewards (everlasting bliss), increase the penalties for non-believers (eternal damnation and torture) and ask us to have absolute faith in order to strengthen our attachment to the religion. Interestingly Buddhism which perhaps pays more attention to happiness (as opposed to other goals) than any other religion does not have the same apocalyptic reward or damnation as other religions.

Children at Kolo Village after they had helped refloat our dinghy

11. Sport, Exercise, Dance, Activities, Hobbies, Pets

In Samoa we found almost every village playing Krikiti all day, practicing for the big tournament in November. Krikiti differs from cricket or baseball in 9 ways: 1. The bat is the size and shape of 3 sided war club, 4 feet long, and is swung just like a war club. 2. It's played on a concrete strip rather than grass 3. The rest of the field is sharp lava rocks, sometimes cow pasture. 4. The players usually play in bare feet. 5. The ball has to be made of rubber, so it floats, as Krikiti is usually played next to the sea and otherwise they lose too many balls - 1 fielder is usually positioned swimming in the sea. 6. The wicket keeper (catcher) bowls (pitches) the next ball back to the hitter at the other end as soon as he has it, (cricket could copy this - it keeps the game much faster). 7. More or less all the men of the village play - grey haired patriarchs swing their war clubs with the village youth. 8. There is no sense of defensive play - each batter has a wild swing at every ball, and usually sends it 60+ metres. 9. The side in the field perform extravagant synchronized handclapping and jigging under the direction of their leader. And one similarity: If the ball hits the stumps or the ball is caught, the batsman is out. Its all great fun, and probably excellent practice (or a substitute) for war.

The more active we are, the happier we are – that at least seems to be the findings, and they are reasonably robust. 3 periods of exercise/week of about 30 minutes/session will, in addition to losing weight, increase our level of happiness by 10-20% provided we do it for at least 6 months. Which begs the question: Why don't more of us do it?

Well, one reason may be lack of knowledge, but another may have to do with evolution – since most of our predecessors HAD to exercise in order to hunt or gather the food and drink they needed to survive, there may not have been any evolutionary benefit in adding happiness as a further reinforcement for this behaviour. It is only as we have become more specialized that we can lead lives which require no more exercise than picking up the car keys, pushing an elevator button, moving a mouse, and operating a keyboard, that this becomes a problem.

So if evolution has not given some of us a feeling of happiness or even 'flow' as we exercise, what can we do about it?

Well, one way is to manipulate exercise into a form which makes it easier to 'get in the flow' or forget ourselves – and this is exactly what dance does, also most forms of active sport. Seen this way sport and dance are a potent blend of social interaction, sex, music and action which gets us moving so naturally that we want to do more, and forget any pain from our muscles. Advertising, marketing, peer pressure can all have positive effects to encourage us to exercise even when we 'don't want to'. Even having a pet seems to make us more active, and indeed having a pet also makes us happier – partly because of the extra activity, partly because of the social interaction (our pet may well be our best friend).

In contrast, living alone, or working alone (or both) not only misses out on friendship, but may also not provide the encouragement to exercise that a group of friends (or having a pet) does. So our apparent preference for living alone may be as maladaptive as the frequent Victorian preference in leisure for large meals and doing very little – because up to that point it had not been possible to do it. Just because we can now live alone does not mean that it is good for us, or will make us happier, any more than doing nothing will. If living alone means that we aren't stimulated to exercise, then there is already a powerful argument that we will not be as happy as we can be.

Massed worshippers, Bali 2006

12. WHAT HAS MOST INFLUENCE ON HOW HAPPY WE ARE?

> The pink lure comes off, and the shimmering stripes on his side running from iridescent blue to steel grey slowly sink into the depths and Intrepid and the Marlin go on our separate ways, both wiser and very much tireder – but with enough adrenalin to last us all a month. Denis is in 7th Heaven.

Let's summarise briefly. Many factors seem to vary with happiness, and these often overlap; while psychological experiments often leave out factors that others find important. Many studies look to see what changes occur at the same time as changes in happiness – correlations – but of course this says nothing about whether they cause happiness or unhappiness.

This is complex. A psychologist called Daniel Nettle recently attempted to collate what has the greatest influence on making us happy (or unhappy). Combining a number of studies, he concluded that the main factors considered one at a time were:

Factor	Variation accounted for
Neurotic/Stable Personality	6-28%
Extrovert/Introvert Personality	2-16%
Other Personality Factors	8-14%
Marital Status (Married)	6%
Higher Social Class	4%
Higher Income	3%
Age (Older)	1%
Sex (Male)	1%

Richard (Lord) Layard in his excellent book on Happiness gave a different summary of the most important 5 factors:

Most important: Family Relationships

Financial Situation

Work

Community and Friends

Health

Layard also noted that Personal Freedom, and Personal Values, although these don't have such a clear direct effect on happiness, are also important. Interestingly, perhaps because he is an economist originally, Layard does not focus on personality and activities, (unless they are included in family relationships or personal values or health). So there is still some disagreement on what are the important factors.

Nettle's table demonstrates some of the uncertainty (a range of between 6 and 28% for Neurotic Personality is hardly precise!), and warns us against focusing on minor detail when even the bigger picture is in such doubt. However, it does confirm the major effect of internal long term factors like our personality, as compared to external things like income, marital status etc. It also reminds us that although the advertising industry tries to persuade us that the secret of happiness lies in many possessions that go with a high income, and a celebrity life style, these have only a little effect; whereas our personality has a much greater effect. In fact, there appears to be a kind of 'set point' determined by our genes which drives how happy we are and are going to be in future.

If we are worrying about questions like whether to change jobs, or downsize or quit work altogether, this is important, because it reminds us that we are not very likely to find the 'solution' to being happy in a change of job or even stopping work altogether. The answer is more likely to lie within us, in a part of our personality that is however very resistant to change, even if we wanted to change it.

So does this mean that a change of job is irrelevant? No, because jobs are much more than 'just' income; and as we have already seen, there are some effects related to external factors which are important. And unlike much of our personality, some of these external factors are ones that we can influence. In other words, we seem to have a frustrating situation where the major factors determining happiness we can't really control; but we can control or at least influence some of the less significant factors. So we have a table like this:

	Big Effect on Happiness	Smaller Effect on Happiness
Easier to change	?	Income, Marital status
Difficult to change	Personality	Male/Female; Age

It would be nice to find some factors that are easy to change and would have a big effect on our happiness. However, life isn't that easy.

It would still seem that we have some options if we want to increase our happiness. Either we can strive to change our income, or marital status or other external factors, which may increase our happiness a bit. Or we can look for some internal ways of looking at the world which may not have quite the same effect as changing our personality, but will at least have some effect.

Are there changes like this? There are, and they are generally contained in the self-help literature, which may explain why they are so popular. So books on 'How to win friends and influence people' or Emotional Intelligence or Neuro Linguistic Programming (NLP), or Cognitive Behavioural Therapy, (CBT) or even Religion (which is a way of changing the way we think about the world) sell well, and help to change the outlook of many people. Will they make us happier? Are there aspects of what we can call positive thinking that can help us to lead a happier and more satisfying life?

We may be a bit cynical or suspicious at times about them, because after all they are usually being 'sold' so it's as well to look at the motives of the person doing the selling. Do they really have our interests at heart, or are they really more concerned with getting rich themselves? However, it does make sense to look for support in thinking about the past, present and future in a positive way and there are ways to help do this.

Marriage, Income and Social Class

Another implication from the table is that when we are considering major decisions like whether to change job, or stop work, we need to look at the combination of Marital Status, Income and Social Class. Although each has a relatively small effect, taken together these do actually account for quite a sizeable variation in happiness, some 13%, similar to either of the Big 2 personality dimensions – and whereas we find it difficult to change our personality, we can sometimes change our income, marital status and to a lesser extent social class very quickly – much of this is within our power.

So for example if the change we are considering involves a significant drop in income, a lowering of our social class (eg from banker to gardener), and perhaps a divorce or separation, then we can predict that by itself this may have a sizeable negative effect on happiness. There will of course be subsequent adaptation, but it is as well to appreciate in advance that this is likely to happen, and that there ideally needs to be other factors to offset this likely loss of happiness. These changes can even lead to depression in people who have not experienced it before. This is not surprising, when we recall that people in the lowest quarter of social class (which is itself partly determined by job) are twice as likely to suffer depression as those in the top quarter.

So if we are considering whether to change job, or to stop work altogether, we should calculate how much our income will reduce, whether it will lower our social class (or status, which is a slightly different variable but still comparable), and whether the change is likely to result in a divorce or separation.

On the positive side, we need to consider what other changes will take place in our life that are likely to affect our happiness. This may include a lessening of anxiety, frustration and stress, (which if we are already fairly high on the anxious, worried neurotic personality scale is likely to have a disproportionate effect on our happiness), fewer hours worked, more variety and more satisfying work, greater sense of being in control, and more opportunities to get into a 'flow' situation where we enjoy what we are doing so much that we lose all track of time.

We should also consider how we will adapt to the changes. Whereas the first day may seem blissful, what will be the effect after 1 month, 1 year, 10 years, or 30 years?

Partly this will depend on how we explain or rationalize the change to ourselves. Women, are more likely to rehearse the changes in their mind, and if the changes are perceived to be bad, this is more likely to lead to depression. Women are also more likely on average than men to attribute the cause of the bad effects to themselves, ('I am not good enough or attractive enough'), and to generalize it ('It will always be like this and won't get better') so again there is a higher chance of becoming depressed.

Of course, only we can answer these questions, but we will make a better informed decision if we are aware of the factors that are likely to play a key role, and the extent to which we can influence them. However, this is not the complete story.

There are 7 ways of thinking that people frequently use to make sense of the world, and to create our 'mental model' of what is going on around us. These are often 'defence mechanisms' we use to make the world seem a better place and to reinforce our sense of being in control of our life. They can affect our happiness, but they also affect the way we make decisions. These defence mechanisms are very important and useful – but if we rely on them to make important decisions in our life, they can seriously mislead us, so we need to be aware of them. This is explored in Part Two.

Part Two:

How to make better Work-Life Decisions

13. How we remember events and how this affects the way we plan for the future

> It still rankles with many Virginians that the South lost the Civil War, (they call it the War of Northern Aggression) and people we talked to in bars – including one whose forefathers came over in 1654 from Hampshire, England – told us at some length that Virginians never lost a battle.

Our memory is a long way from being an accurate recollection of past events. Since we often base our decisions and plans for the future on those (often inaccurate) memories, this is important. Our memory of events is largely determined by the peak episode and how it ended. So a holiday or a conference will often be remembered by one significant occurrence (good or bad) and how the event ended. Some of the experiments in this area are by Nobel Prize winning psychologist, Daniel Kahneman.

Our memory is not a movie we access and which plays back scenes that happened to us. In practice it would be more accurate to describe memory as re-fabricating from prominent parts of the actual event – often the peak and the end. So we use this to remember how we felt about any event, and may well miss out whole days. Try to remember your holiday one year ago, or your last job. Think of the events you can remember clearly, then work out how many days you were there. Chances are that you noted a few peak memories, and how it ended. Yet during all this period, you were going through ups and downs, you were happy and unhappy, but the likelihood is that this is all summarized in your memory as a few events, the whole probably being coloured by how you felt at the peak and when it ended. This may provide an accurate estimation of our happiness overall – but it also may not.

We may remember the worst event in a holiday, (perhaps a major argument) and the car which broke down on the return journey. The rest of the holiday may actually have been very pleasant, and if asked on each of the other days we would have given it high ratings in terms of happiness – but in memory the re-fabrication will be largely negative.

Why does this matter? It matters because the way we usually plan for the future depends on our present mood, and our anticipation of future events and activities which are based on our memories which are highly selective. So we may have a really bad day at the office in a week which ends badly. We will probably give a very low value to working; and the pleasure to be gained by stopping may seem extreme.

But we are probably being unduly influenced by the peak/end phenomenon, and a more balanced appreciation would come out with a very different answer. Or we may have finished a holiday, during which we had one particularly special day when the weather was magnificent and everything seemed to just 'flow' effortlessly, and the holiday finished with a wonderful party which just seemed perfect. Returning to work seems so hard and our memory of these days of leisure may seem wonderfully attractive.

But chances are that the holiday also contained some not so good times when things broke, there were arguments, we were bored, and people drank too much (never ourselves of course). Using our re-fabricated memory of this holiday as a proxy for stopping work may give a misleading impression of the bliss that we think awaits us.

We need to know about this general principle if we are to make better decisions. Because if we are pre-warned about this effect, and especially if we are asked to pay particular attention to a particular aspect (like the weather for example) then this will not be subject to the broad generalizations that can lead to poor judgments. For example, people were asked to estimate whether moving from the Mid-West states to California would make them any happier. People in both California and the Mid-West estimated that moving to California would make them happier, and that people in California are happier than in the mid-West. Probably the subjects were thinking of the weather and the ocean and the good things of life that are most often associated with California.

But in fact when the experimenters measured the happiness of people in California and the Mid-West they found happiness to be the same. Presumably the same people who focused on the attributes that are associated with California (sun, ocean, glamour etc) didn't take into account the less well publicized aspects of living in California like crowded roads, pollution, intense status competition, cost of housing, blackouts etc. If people based a decision on whether to quit their job and move to California to be happy, on their imagined impression of California, the chances are that they would be misguided and end up less happy than before. This has clear implications for the decision to change jobs, or to quit altogether.

This is a trick played on us every day by Advertisers and Public Relations and Lobby firms. They know that their product or firm or business has various positive (+) aspects and other negative (−) aspects. If we can be persuaded to focus on the positive aspects, then this will probably crowd out our appreciation of the negative aspects and our general impression will be positive. So they work hard to make these features seem important, and we will often incorporate these features into our memory of the product or business and create a warm glow when we think of it which may be quite illusory. Brand image in fact. For example, if they want us to buy a cruise, they will try to make these points 'important' ie the things that will spring to mind when we think of a cruise:

Exotic locations

Cordon Bleu Food

Glamorous passengers

Entertainment

Now the following may also be features of a cruise, but the advertiser would prefer that we did not consider these as important:

Sea sickness

3rd world destinations and poverty

Restricted accommodation

Rushed tours ashore

Fortunately, when our attention is drawn to a particular feature, then our judgments and memory start to become more precise, and we 'factor out' some or all of the irrelevant positive factors. So for example when people were asked on a sunny day how happy there were, they generally rated themselves as happy, whereas if it was raining, they were less happy. However, if the interviewer asked (on the telephone) 'By the way what is the weather like where you are?' then the effect of weather disappeared.

So we can help our brains to make better decisions by breaking the features down into smaller dimensions and paying attention to each one separately.

We are being continually bombarded by events and media, the government and our employing organisation all of which are competing for our attention, particularly in the way they relate to major purchasing or life style changing decisions. In some ways we should welcome this competition for our attention, because it lies at the heart of our free society. But that does not make it balanced or representative or right for us. Only we can decide that, and all too often this is not a conscious decision.

Making wise decisions

There is a paradox; the freer people are to choose, the more they are able to make unwise decisions regarding their future. This may be partly because of information overload, or a poor memory of past events and feelings, or not being aware of the factors involved. In the end many decisions are swayed more by current mood than by a rational thought process. And while this may be satisfying emotionally in the short term, it may have far reaching negative consequences, probably unintended.

The way to avoid this is thought: getting clearer about what we want and the probable consequences. But if our increasing wealth and income, or simply lack of time makes us blasé about this, then wealth and stress may sow the seeds of some fairly disastrous decisions.

The increasing complexity and rate of change of our modern technological and financial world makes it increasingly difficult for most people to make the best decisions for themselves at the same time that governments are privatizing and increasing choice in everything from telephones to pensions. This overload often means that our decisions are far from best for us.

Many decisions on how happy we are, are significantly influenced by our minute by minute mood. So if we are feeling cheerful, we tend to report that our goods are reliable, that the political scene is positive, that the future is bright. Conversely if we are feeling a bit down, we will be much more negative about all these things. This was tested in a shopping mall where someone went around doing small favours for people, then a minute or so later they were asked by an experimenter about a range of items. In each case the reported feelings were more positive following the small favour.

Even finding a small coin (10c, about 5p) brightens our mood and will (incredibly) affect decisions. This is actually a very useful evolutionary adaptation mechanism. Imagine that life is tough, very tough, the saber tooth tiger has just eaten our best friend, and the berries that the household relies on have failed. It would be easy to slip into a depression, and to refuse to go outside the cave. But if our mood can be brightened by even a small gesture, our child for example giving us a smile, or finding a small piece of food we had missed, this will have significant survival consequences if it motivates to get up, go out, and resume the hunting and gathering.

So resilience and adaptation are important. This is explored in the next chapter.

Old Sa'ana, Yemen before the current conflict
2007

14. Adaptation, Mid-life crisis, and how we take things for granted and cope

> It felt really strange when we arrived in the Marquesas – we were all a bit scared I think, after 3500 miles of Pacific nothingness there were cars and houses and people. We had adapted to life in mid Pacific, now we had to adapt back again to 'normal' life.

Our decisions on future events are likely to be flawed, because our memory of past events is highly selective. But our imagined future may also be wrong in another way. In a number An experimenter asked people to imagine what it would be like to be a paraplegic, (in a wheel chair) or to win a million dollars. Unsurprisingly the subjects estimated that becoming a paraplegic would make people very unhappy, and winning a million dollars would make them very happy. But in fact, when people are in just this situation (who have become paraplegic or won a million dollars) and are asked how happy they are, the answers are very different. The paraplegics rate themselves a little lower than the general population, but by such a small amount as to be almost negligible; and lottery winners seem to revert back to their previous level of happiness within a few weeks of winning.

What we have failed to take into account is the adaptation that people make when significant changes happen to them. We are not passive observers of the world about us, we actively choose what to look at and what sort of a mental model to make. Our frame of reference changes, so that we start to compare ourselves with a different set of people. So the lottery winner may indeed be happy because she has won one million dollars. But soon she will find that whereas previously a dinner at the local restaurant was rated as a very good night out, now it has to be dinner at a 5-star prime steak restaurant to achieve the same level of happiness. What has happened is that she has adapted. Similarly, the paraplegic, after the awful shock and recovery process, finds that there are still things to enjoy in life like friends and communications, and likewise they adapt to their new situation. This is especially admirable and shows the real resilience and self-reliance that we have inherited from our hunter gatherer ancestors (if we gave up when injured or ill, we were unlikely to survive long enough to parent children and pass on our genes).

However, when people are making judgments about the future, they consistently underestimate the likely adaptation that they will make to the new circumstances.

The relevance of this to work and life decisions is clear. We may think of stopping work and imagine ourselves as if we were on holiday – and in one sense we will be – but very quickly we will adapt, and our actual thoughts are likely to be very different in retirement from those on holiday. In other words, our estimation of how we will feel when we stop work is likely to be very different from reality – unless we work very hard at the estimating process.

In fact, this adaptation process is even wider than us as an individual. If everyone adapts in a certain way, then our decisions are also affected by others – so affluence may lead to increasing property values, or congestion, or increasing expectations of the levels of goods and services required for a normal life.

And there is another factor at work - around age 40 there is something that Ericsson called the mid-life crisis, (by the way, he did not mean a danger, rather a critical time to re-evaluate our lives). We need to make a mid-course correction – where we have got to, what we have (part possessions, but more importantly our talents, skills, values, friends, interests, abilities as well as the things we do not have), because the approach that has worked for us up to age 40 is unlikely to be the best approach from 40 to 60.

We may well find that our hair is balding, our waist is expanding, our prowess in speed, power and agility in sports is waning, and our sexual ability is not what it was. We may also find that as we lose our ability to have children (except with complicated procedures), and our children go to school, we start to question who we are, what we should be doing, whether we define ourselves more by partnership or independence, and worry more about our looks.

Both men and women may try to compensate for this by extra exercise, personal trainers, drugs, cosmetic procedures, diets, sexual adventures and marathons to prove to ourselves that we still look young and attractive or at least can still get a buzz from new adventures, and most people go down this route – some for longer, some for shorter.

But in the end this looking back, trying to hang onto youth becomes counter-productive and artificial even to our friends, and we need to start working out our adaptation – our mid-course correction to take account of who we really are and where we want to be. This means changing our reference group – the people we compare ourselves with. And we are likely to worry far more about people close to us than remote cases – they are more 'salient' or important and more noticeable.

Because at age 40 we are only just over one quarter of the way into adulthood. We have a realistic expectation of living until we are 90, so having worked for 20 years, we have another 50 ahead of us. How we plan these years, what we really want to achieve with all the skills and resources we have acquired in our first years of work – our personal strategy in fact - is going to be genuinely critical for us, and whilst we may want to ignore it, it is not going to go away.

This does not need super intelligence. If rational thought really was the secret of happiness, then intelligent people would be the happiest. In fact, there is almost no effect at all of intelligence on happiness. So whether we are super intelligent or super stupid or somewhere in between we are just as likely and have just as good an opportunity to be happy or unhappy.

Donating fresh water to an Indonesian Fishing Boat underway
2006

15. Why we value things that we lose more highly than those we gain

> Denis kids me about our wind/water generator, and asks why I keep repairing it. Well, by now it's been with us for over 30,000 miles, so it's like an old friend; it may have faults, but at least I know what they are.

Try these thought experiments:

Imagine that a friend borrows your car and damages it so badly that it is a write off. The insurance pays up, but how do you feel?

Or:

You are on holiday, and someone steals your wallet or jewelry or mobile phone or your home is broken into and personal goods stolen. Insurance pays, but is this the whole story?

Or:

You have a piece of land, or some other asset. Someone comes up to you and offers to buy it for its market value. This is the 'correct' value, but do you agree to sell?

Or:

You receive a bonus, then about 18 months later you receive a tax demand for 40% of it. Compare this to the situation where you receive the bonus with the tax already deducted.

Psychologists are often accused of trying to prove the obvious, and this is no exception. We tend to place a higher value on things we own then lose, than strict market valuation. This 'sentimental value' has been demonstrated a number of times, for example when people were given a pretty china cup, and then the experimenter tried to buy it back from them, the people asked for more than double the amount they were prepared to pay for it in the first place. In fact, there seems to be a fairly reliable formula:

Value of something we own then lose = 2.5 x Its Market Value.

In other words, the person buying would have to offer 2.5 times its value to persuade us that it is worth parting with it, unless there are other benefits in the equation. We seem to tie up our self-esteem with goods we have chosen, the more so if we have worked hard or parted with money to get them. We like what we chose because we chose it, and if we lose it, it gains even more value. So regrets at losing something are more than twice as powerful as the joy of having it.

This would imply that if we have a company car, and have to give it up when we leave, then we are likely to find the loss significantly worse than the actual monetary value of the car. There may be many perks or advantages in our work which we may not even be aware of. But if we have to give them up we may well find that their loss causes us significant distress, or 'happiness loss' – far more than we might have anticipated before we left.

To some extent we are the victims of our own adaptation that we discussed in the previous chapter. When we first receive some new benefit or perk at work, it initially is motivating and exciting, but after a while we get used to having it, it becomes 'part of the furniture', and far from it motivating us, we come to take it for granted, and when asked, may not even remember it. Even worse, we are likely to regard it as 'essential' after a while. As we saw, our view of what income we 'need' tends to increase as our total income goes up.

However, when we are suddenly faced with the prospect of leaving, we may suddenly come to realise that we are about to lose a number of benefits or possessions – perhaps a car, loans, private health care, technology support, private education, continuing professional development, laptops, pc's and phones, business or 1st class air travel, membership of a gym, free phone calls, attending sports events, secretarial support, legal advice, insurance, to say nothing of losing friends and business contacts, and that losing them will be very significant to us and our own sense of self-esteem.

This is illustrated by the lengths some people go to try to negotiate continuation of some benefits when they are stopping work or changing jobs. (Just read about the benefits CEO's try to take with them when they leave). This tendency to over value items we are about to lose is an important one, and in making a judgment on any change of job, we need to pay more attention to what we are losing, than to what we are gaining – at least in terms of our own happiness.

This is particularly so if these items are likely to be ones that we frequently notice –especially if they keep on being drawn to our attention. For example, if we move from a job in the city to one in the country, then having to give up our Company 4x4 may be especially important because we are likely to find ourselves in situations where we need 4-wheel drive and huge horsepower. We may also have to give up airport lounge facilities or tickets to a sporting event or secretarial support so that our week is organised for us. When we go on holiday with our partner, or see the game on TV instead of live from a hospitality box, or arrange our own diary or pc this aspect of the loss is likely to be particularly important.

One common tactic is to try to avoid situations that stimulate this sense of loss. So we may avoid car show rooms or advertisements with the model of car that we have had to give up, and even emphasise the bad points it had; or ignore the sporting event that we used to be able to go to. Our friends may call this 'sour grapes' but in fact it is a perfectly valid and useful emotional defence mechanism – provided we do not allow ourselves to subsequently make judgments based on these artificially engineered memories and values.

So it is unwise to focus on regaining what we have lost, because our sense of loss is causing some emotional distress. In romance there is even a name for this, 'marrying on the rebound'. Instead we need to be aware of this phenomenon of overvaluing that which we have had to give up, and review all the options open to us, which may well offer more and better opportunities than trying to regain the past.

Gambling

Of course, there are exceptions to this sense of loss. One of the most common exceptions is gambling – why do people bet when (in most cases) on average they lose money? The money gambled may often be a significant portion of our income or wealth. There are 4 factors that make us ignore our losses:

1. An inability to delay gratification – rather than wait the years it may take to accumulate a fortune by working, there is a temptation, particularly when in an aroused state, to take a chance on getting the fortune now.
2. Inattention – particularly when we gamble using a credit card or even cash, the value to us may not seem like very much – it's just a signature or Pin on an electronic screen. Casinos reinforce this by using plastic chips, which are even further removed from real cash. If we had to gamble with our car, or house, or favoured piece of art, then we might not be quite so keen to gamble.
3. Our self-esteem – we are persuaded that our judgment is so good we should back our own judgment.
4. The partial reinforcement effect where irregular winnings, (compared to predictable regular winnings), produce behaviour that is very stubborn and ingrained and continues even when the rewards (winnings) stop.

To help us ignore our losses and continue gambling, the casino or betting shop use these 4 factors to make the gamble as unobtrusive as possible (maybe an internet account or credit card); winnings as obvious and immediate as possible; and to boost the self-esteem of the winner ('You were really smart to predict all 6 correct numbers!). Think of the huge cheques presented often on TV to the winners of lotteries, (15 minutes of fame), the effort to arrange not just large prizes but gigantic prizes, and the promotion of long odds bets which win almost at random, or even the clinking of slot machines as they dispense at irregular intervals hundreds of coins, watched by by-standers.

These insights give clues to some of the ways that Governments try to discourage gambling, for example not allowing ATM's in casinos (so you at least have to change cash for chips), limiting alcohol, limiting or delaying the size of pay-outs and where possible reducing their impact, and allowing cooling off periods. Of course, when governments or charities benefit from gambling (through betting tax or lottery good causes) there is a conflict of interest and the limitations are often completely side-lined.

But people with special appetites for arousal do still make risky decisions. Whatever the reason, gambling with our career or when to stop work or any other major work life decision is unlikely to have good outcomes. We may overestimate the odds of winning because we are so aroused, and the prize seems so attractive. Or we may operate on mood, and skip the rational thought process that calculates the odds altogether and just focus on the prize. Or we may be searching for a sense of personal control which life does not give us most of the time. Or we may think that we are more skilled than the average person (which most people do), in which case it is consistent to take a risk because our self-esteem is tied up with it, and we genuinely believe that we will on average win. This striving for consistency is the subject of the next chapter.

Nicky and Jill on a donkey cart, Suakin, Sudan
2007

16. How we try to get our memories and values consistent

> The Bastille Day 14th July celebrations in Bora Bora near Tahiti in mid Pacific were in full swing with some 100 performers pounding drums, wiggling hips and flexing muscles in synchronised splendour. Parents, small children, dogs, transvestite males (who weren't sure whether to wiggle their hips or flex their muscles), watched from the side. These celebrations commemorate the treaties bringing Polynesia under French rule. Somehow the French have persuaded the Society Islanders to celebrate their subjugation (to the French) on the same day that the French celebrate their own freedom from a tyrannical king.

Our memory is more like a re-fabricated model of highly selective cameos of our past, than a simple video or series of pictures. However, there is another effect also at work. We like to think that our behaviour and decisions are consistent with our values and self-esteem. If they are inconsistent, we use a variety of methods to restore consistency.

To take a simple example, suppose that we pride ourselves on our knowledge in some area, football for example, or local history. We make a prediction to a large number of people, that Manchester United will win, or that this garden was designed by Capability Brown, the famous landscape designer. Then it turns out that Manchester United lose and a respected authority declares that the garden was NOT designed by Capability Brown. We now have a problem, because the evidence and our sense of good judgment in this area are not consistent.

Whilst we could just shrug this off, in many cases we will make strenuous efforts to re-establish consistency. For example, we may declare that if we had known that a particular player was injured, then of course we would have predicted that Manchester United would lose. Or had we been told that the garden had subsequently been remodelled after its original design, then of course we would have known that

Capability Brown could not have designed it. Or we may even decide to redefine our specialism, so that our predictions only apply to home games, or to Capability Brown Gardens designed before 1775, or only in England.

This even applies in our relationships with our friends. Suppose our best friend likes to think of themselves as a keen and knowledgeable art critic. She is a passionate admirer of the work of a new modern artist, and invites us to the artist's first exhibition where our friend has already bought one of the works for a large sum of money. We enter the exhibition, and our first reaction is that they are awful. Our friend advances on us, says how great the exhibition is, and asks our opinion. What do we say?

What is happening is that we place a high value on our friend, and know that she places a high value on her artistic judgment. Yet the works she admires we find awful – low value. This is clearly inconsistent. So we consciously or unconsciously try to find ways to synchronise the situation, to make it consistent.

We may decide that the young artist is indeed talented – but only in a few works including the one our friend has bought; or we can explain that the gallery have hung the works in the wrong way. This is not just being polite – it's likely that we find it difficult to have contradictory ideas in our head at the same time.

In art this may just about work, but suppose our friend comes home with a new car. We initially think it is awful, but clearly they are in love with it, and have spent a lot of money on it. The likelihood is that we will try to find good points about the car, and indeed will probably come to value the car more, just because our friend thinks so much of it. This is exactly what advertisers do - get a high profile and admired celebrity to buy their product because people who admire the celebrity will also value items that the celebrity has chosen. Or they may show beautiful actors that we admire driving the car, so that we link the car with these positive values.

We even seem to do this unconsciously, and this leads to some very powerful consequences. Suppose an organisation has a selection process that is long, difficult nasty and expensive; and another organisation has a selection process that is quick, comfortable, easy and costs nothing. Which do you think would be rated as the best organisation by the participants after they had passed the entry process?

The surprising answer is the organisation which has the long nasty difficult expensive initiation. The reasoning presumably goes like this: 'I am a sensible and relatively clever person. If I have gone through a nasty and difficult experience, then the outcome (being a member of this organisation) MUST be really good, otherwise I have just done something very stupid'.

By contrast the person who has had an easy entry process will be thinking that if it is that easy to get into, then it can't be very special, along the lines of the comment by Grouch Marx that "I wouldn't want to be a member of any club which would have me as a member".

However, those people who fail the entry process, are likely to undervalue the difficult organisation, or speak disparagingly about the ridiculous selection or recruitment process, thus retaining their consistency and own sense of self-esteem. (If we still think the organisation is good, then we had better think that its selection process is inaccurate).

Another example is smoking. In Canada, some provinces increased taxes on smoking. One might think that smokers in these provinces would become less happy. But in fact they reported increased happiness. Presumably since they were spending even more money on smoking, this becomes especially obvious, and they have to report even higher levels of satisfaction if they are to be consistent in still smoking.

This need for consistency (its original name is cognitive dissonance) can affect many decisions. For example, people who had taken a difficult course to produce professional quality photographs were given the choice of keeping just one photograph. Others on the course were told that they could keep one, but could swap it later for another photograph. The people who could not swap valued their photo more highly than the other group. The reasoning presumably is that since this photo is the only tangible product of this difficult course, then since I went to considerable effort and time to complete it, I should place a high value on the only tangible result of it. By contrast, those who could swap the photo did not need to place such a high value on it, since they could get another. If we have spent a lot of our money buying a car, house or other object, it is consistent to place an especially high value on it, more even than the market value.

There is even evidence that we like those who we have helped more than we like those who help us. If we have invested in helping someone, it is consistent to believe that they are 'valuable', whereas if we need help, this is consistent with a feeling of low self-esteem.

Rationalising Inconsistency

This need for consistency is a leading cause for our tendency to 'compartmentalise' our thinking, so that apparently inconsistent behaviour becomes consistent because of the special circumstances we are in. For example, we may note that Americans are very generous and sociable when in what they perceive to be social situations, but hard and demanding in situations they define as commercial. This apparently inconsistent behaviour (generous v. demanding) becomes quite consistent when the situations are 'compartmentalised'.

This is important when we come to make critical work life decisions, because it is so powerful that unless we are aware of it, we will make some very poor decisions.

This compartmentalization can provide a rationalization for selfish behaviour, which on the face of it would be inconsistent with our stated values. So a substandard CEO may propose himself an especially large pay rise 'not because I need the money but because if I don't, then everyone else beneath me will not be able to have a pay rise either, and we won't motivate the younger staff if they don't have a target to aim at'. Some politicians are particularly good at 'serving the people' by appropriating huge sums, private jets, large staffs and palatial houses. Believers in a religion may cope with persecution by dramatically increasing the rewards for true believers (everlasting bliss for example), so that it is consistent to endure troubles.

The need for consistency can also lead us to over-value a particular job. The need for consistency occurs when we have had to undergo difficult or stressful experiences – like accountancy or University exams, or a particularly rigorous evaluation or interview or project. Because it is so hard, this leads us to overvalue the result. So if our work is particularly stressful and pressured we restore consistency by increasing the value we place on being in work and in this particular job. Consistency, by creating a coping mechanism can keep people in jobs they probably would be better off leaving. Since it may often be unconscious, it is particularly important to be aware of it when we are making work and life decisions.

Old fishing port of Suakin, Sudan

17. Self Reliance

> Only about 100 yachts cross the Pacific each year, and we have seen some of the biggest ones: 80 -100 feet plus, crews of 12 and daily operating budgets in excess of US$6000. Tiny Bubbles is 24 feet long, no motor, 2 people on board, left the USA with $250, and 2/3 way across in Samoa still have $170 left. They seem happier than almost anyone else we have met.

In 1840, Ralph Waldo Emerson wrote a classic book called Self Reliance. Although only 30 pages long, it forged part of the American ideal of individualism. Emerson thought self-reliance crucial and revelled in nature, so in part he advocated the self-reliant American frontiersman, but also a spirit of non-conformity, individuals achieving their own potential. Emerson was not in favour of running around trying to improve or better the world or even giving to good causes until we find a place in the world that seems right to us. 'Nothing can bring you peace but yourself. Nothing can bring you peace but the triumph of principles' he wrote. 'Insist on yourself, never imitate. Your own gift you can present every moment with the cumulative force of a whole life's cultivation'. Or as we might say nowadays 'I did it my way'. If we have been working for a large organisation, the need for self reliance when we stop working for them is clear.

In terms of the present day, we may think of self-reliance as not being dependant on big organisations, or even lots of support services, but rather being able to deal with the world on our own terms. Sailing is a particularly suitable way to explore this, although of course there are many other ways, getting back to nature in general being favoured. Although few of us actually design and build our own boat, and with GPS and mobile and satellite phones we are not completely alone in the world; a yacht requires a lot of self-reliance (unless you hire a skipper and engineer and large crew). Sailing both provides the requirement for self-sufficiency, as well as the satisfaction (or happiness) that comes from achieving it.

Of course there are other ways to develop and challenge our own self-reliance – and increasingly people are doing this by attempting to climb Everest or ride the length of the Americas, or Africa or the Paris/Dacca rally or running a farm or small business. Central to all this is the acquisition of enough skills to be able to look after ourselves – for only in this way can we be reasonably independent of the conventions of society, and feel free to do our own thing.

This is clearly a long term project – we don't suddenly wake up one morning and realize we are self-reliant. But all the time we are reliant on other people or organisations, we are effectively not in control of our lives, and are less likely to feel happy or contented. Of course we can push this too far – often it is good to work with others; and to fight off people who are trying to help can be counterproductive, and downright rude and maladaptive. And sometimes using a contractor or professional makes sense if our time is limited, or the skills needed are so complex that there is no other option.

When we are in a team, often a few individuals horde the available work, and do it themselves, which of course ensures that they develop their skills more and the others in the team do not – even though on the face of it they are having an easy time. This is often the case where expatriates or experts are supposed to develop local staff. The easy way is for the expatriate to do the work, and allow or encourage the local staff to sit back and enjoy life. But this perpetuates the reliance of the local staff on the expatriate – which may be precisely what the expatriate wants.

But if we have skills and resources to chart our own course, we are likely to be happier and more satisfied. We can never be self-reliant in all areas. We are unlikely to be able to perform major heart surgery, or even to make a complex repair on a diesel engine or pump. (The key difference between the engine and the heart being of course is that we can usually stop the engine before we try to repair it). But the skills we have act a bit like wealth, to enable us to be free of as many restrictions as possible, so that we can do what we want.

A clever set of experiments 30 years ago demonstrated that we want what we cannot have (no surprise this perhaps), so we will always want more than we have. What was surprising was how malleable this effect was. The sheer act of restricting access to some food, drink or activity meant that the food drink or activity, even if it had been completely neutral before, became valued. So if we want someone to do something, sometimes the first thing is to forbid them from doing it. Straightaway they are likely to start demanding to be allowed to do it. Masters of Protocol or 'Etiquette' have known this for ages, and restrict access in order to make it more valuable.

Self-reliance requires discipline; skills that can be used in future; and making commitments. We have mechanisms that reinforce self-reliance when temptation looms. These may be household budgets, the priority given to education (which can cost large sums at a time when there are many other ways to spend it), and on commitments like marriage where sexual behaviour is controlled (eg avoiding or minimizing affairs outside marriage). These are all ways people seek to bolster their self-discipline and self-reliance by rituals and by social mechanisms, as well as by laws. General de Gaulle was President of France when he decided to give up smoking. His method was simple – he announced to everyone that he would stop on a specific day. The loss of face and damage to his image of self-reliance would have been huge had he smoked again. He didn't.

This discipline to reinforce self-reliance is even used in governments. Most US states have provisions that require their state governments to balance income and spending. A bill to enforce this on the US Federal Government only failed by one vote. These are mechanisms which recognise that temptation is always with us to 'fudge' issues, to be swayed by momentary moods (or elections or opinion polls), and we need to have processes designed when we are being coldly rational to help us control these impulses which may hit when we are aroused or agitated. Individuals may use the same budgeting processes.

Laws against corruption are another example of this sort of discipline. The whole concept of markets so loved by economists is based on the assumption of arm's length transactions, unswayed by personal relationships, however much this is demonstrated to be a long way from the real state of affairs.

So self-reliance in the form of resources and skills that enable us to chart our own path, and to decide what we want to do for better or worse, is an important ingredient in the happiness recipe – particularly if we are thinking in terms of long term contentment. But self-reliance can also lead to failure – indeed frequently will as we develop our skills. This is covered in the next chapter.

How about this as a description of self-reliance?

If you can keep your head when all about you
Are losing theirs and blaming it on you.
If you can trust yourself when all men doubt you
But make allowance for their doubting too.
If you can wait and not be tired of waiting
Or being lied about, don't deal in lies.
Or being hated, don't give way to hating
And don't look too good, nor talk too wise.
If you can dream – and not make dreams your master
If you can think – and not make thoughts your aim.
If you can meet with Triumph and Disaster
And treat these two imposters just the same.
If you can make one heap of all your winnings
And risk it on one turn of pitch and toss.
And lose and start again at your beginnings
And never breathe a word about your loss.
If you can talk with crowds and keep your virtue
Or walk with Kings – nor lose your common touch.
If neither foes nor loving friends can hurt you
If all men count with you, but none too much.
If you can fill the unforgiving minute
With sixty seconds worth of distance run
Yours is the Earth and everything that's in it
And –which is more – you'll be a Man my son!
Rudyard Kipling, 'If'

(If you prefer a less masculine last line, insert 'you'll know it's all well done'.)

Following Great Happy through the Suez Canal,
with American Warships behind

18. Failure

> Suave (from Sydney) is here, sea water got into their oil during the passage, and they arrived with no engine. Another yacht only arrived thanks to our Galapagos radio net – her rudder almost fell off in mid Pacific (it dropped 2 feet), Another yacht arrived with a dead engine, another tore the track off their mast, and on yet another the skipper and crew were hardly talking and each thought the other was trying to kill them. Long passages take a significant toll on boats and people!

Many major decisions in life and work are precipitated by failure, and sometimes the consequence of our decisions is failure, so it is important to be aware how failure affects us.

It may seem strange to write about failure when we are addressing the issue of what makes us happy or contented, but how we address failures is crucial in determining whether we will be happy or contented. Partly this comes down to self-reliance, and not giving up, using the skills and resources we do have (rather than just wishing we had something more) to solve the problems we encounter. Failures or potential failures can be due to things or people, and it's surprisingly easy to drop into the frame of mind that thinks 'things' are actively trying to do us down ('this computer is just crashing to spite me' etc.) or conspiracy theories ('they' are out to get me). This can be affected by the culture we live in – Japanese society for example works on the principle that objects have 'soul', so even broken needles are buried.

Hassles and relatively minor annoyances in our daily living can have a disproportionately adverse effect on happiness. Up market brands exploit this by promising reliability, even to a level beyond that necessary. How we cope with these minor hassles influences our level of happiness – if we view them as either failures by ourselves, or proof that the 'world is against us', then we may well become unhappy, whereas if we regard them as part of living, then they will have less effect. Interestingly, if we aim for perfection then the inevitable minor hassles may have a larger effect than they need – so perfection, whilst a necessary standard for us to adopt in certain situations is not a wise one to adopt in most cases.

But even if we shake off any thoughts that the world is against us, a whole set of problems in work or sailing or leisure or whatever we are doing is likely to involve other people. In sailing this often comes down to authorities, who demand paperwork or documentation that we don't have, delay or refuse permission to do something, or charge absurdly high amounts for trivial things. It's important to recognise that this is going to happen, and the fact of it happening is not our failure, but that we are probably going to have to negotiate our way out of it.

Best Alternative To a Negotiated Agreement

There are many approaches to negotiating, but the interaction with happiness seems to particularly focus on BATNA or Best Alternative To a Negotiated Agreement, because this is the best way to avoid the helplessness of dealing with a Kafkaesque monopoly bureaucracy. We know the feeling of helplessness when we are dealing with a monopoly supplier who doesn't seem to care. BATNA helps us to work out what is the alternative to a negotiated settlement, so that we feel more in control, more self-reliant. So if authorities do not agree a permit unless we meet some conditions, we have to consider what the alternatives are, eg changing our plans to avoid the need for the permit.

To arrive at a negotiated settlement, consider what differences there are in the value each side places on the items under negotiation. Most successful conclusions will depend on each side getting items they value highly, but which the other party does not. For example, management may value productivity, reliability and quality most, workers may value pay most. Authorities may value order and saving face, sailors may value freedom more.

Learned Helplessness

Part of the importance of failure is the way we explain it to ourselves. Psychologists (for example Professor Martin Seligman who started experiments on learned helplessness in 1960's and now is a prominent researcher in positive psychology) demonstrate that there are 4 ways to explain failure:

We can either internalize what we think is the reason for the failure ('It was my fault') or externalize it ('They caused the problem'). And we can think of the failure as general ('It's always going to be like this') or a one-off (This won't happen again).

Explanations of Problems, Failures etc

	Internal	External
One off	I caused this problem but I will learn from it and won't do it again	They caused this problem but its history now
General	I always cause problems	They always cause problems like this and always will

People who are depressed tend to regard failures as internal and general ('I was to blame, and it will probably happen again'), and allow this to generate guilt or shame, whereas the alternative explanation (It was caused by others or 'things', and is unlikely to happen again) is much more likely to produce a happy, positive and contented frame of mind. So for example people seem to be much more upset if they feel they have been treated unfairly (with the implication that this will happen again). Inequality in societies is a major factor affecting happiness, and general external explanations can lead to all sorts of prejudice, discrimination, blame, mob violence and worse.

Conversely, if something good happens, the explanation that 'I made this a success and there is no reason why it shouldn't happen again' is more likely to result in a happy mental outlook than 'I was just lucky this time'.

Explanations of Success

	Internal	External
One off	I made this success happen	They made this success happen
General	I always create successful outcomes	They are always successful

Of course it is not as easy as that – but there is plenty of evidence that we can control or at least influence how we remember or react to success or failures – and one way is likely to make us happier or more contented.

The external explanation can include the word 'We', in which case we share the explanation of success or failure, and spread around the elation or gloom. Government, Big Business, even TV News may be the unwitting recipient of such 'externalising' of the cause of bad events. If we explain such bad events as being caused by 'them' then of course our trust in 'them' is going to reduce – and trust in government has reduced from about 40% to about 12%, trust in Business Leaders from 50% to about 15% and even in TV News from about 35% to 25%. So how we explain events affects our level of trust.

These explanations matter because when we do encounter failure, the time spent blaming ourselves inevitably takes away time available for solving the problem, or working out an alternative way ahead. It may even blind us to the possibilities inherent in the situation. So if an engine breaks, then blaming ourselves or even someone else for choosing this particular type of engine is unlikely to be productive (beyond a mental note to take this into account next time we choose an engine).

The purpose of advertising is often not to create satisfaction (excitement), but to actively cause dissatisfaction (lack of contentment), and to foment this into a general movement (think of word of mouth advertising for example) so that we try to correct this by buying whatever is being advertised. We are continually challenged with being inadequate, unreliable or not having enough status, and how we respond to this is going to be a powerful indicator of how happy we are.

Of course, there are cases where we would rather that people are not universally happy. If the problem is a near miss accident, perhaps on the road, or in the office, or a near failure of an engine or piece of equipment, or even worse an aircraft technician or air traffic controller or surgeon, we would rather the person responsible is not devoting themselves to staying happy by reassuring themselves that 'This problem is not my fault and it won't happen again'. In other words, we see that the pursuit of happiness is not necessarily such a desirable goal from a work point of view – at least not without quite a lot of conditions and looking at a suitable time frame. Or to put it another way which brings out the evolutionary connections:

> 'It's survival of the fittest, not survival of the happiest'

So sometimes pain or unhappiness is good for us, and even if they are not good for us as an individual, then they may be good for us as a species – otherwise why did we evolve as we have? What is good for the individual is not always what is best for the group, and vice versa. Adam Smith's great insight was that individual striving for personal gain also benefits the wider group. This is not always the case, and it is the conditions and limits to this that are central to business, team effectiveness, politics and well-being in general. This is explored in more detail in the Chapter 'Are Happychondriacs a threat to Society?

What we do see, is that different types of personality or mental outlook may be best suited to different types of job and explanations for failure – for example an entertainer when faced with a failure (if she or he is good) may make it into a joke, for example if a joke falls flat, they may turn this into a joke itself. Whereas if we were looking for an internal auditor or inspector, we might want someone who worries a great deal about failures, what caused them and how they could be avoided. Great artists often have a manic depressive/bipolar character which may be why they achieve great heights but also plumb the lowest depths of despair and perceived failure.

This interaction of personality and job or career is vitally important in life and career choice and in selection of people for jobs ranging up the very highest level, which explains why psychologists are often used in selection processes.

Internalising the explanation for failures can even lead to suicide in extreme cases – young women attempt suicide twice as often as men, perhaps because they explain failures in terms of their own fault. But young men are 6 times more likely to succeed, so have a suicide rate 3 times higher than young women, and the suicide rate for men is higher than women at all age ranges – and is increasing especially in young men. So how we explain failure is important, as is the presence of friends as already described.

There is one other way that is likely to make us unhappier when we deal with failures – that is when we try to hide them. This adds a level of stress ('what will we do if people find out?') to what is already a difficult enough situation. That is not to say that we should publicise our failures, but it is not worth trying to hide them either – at least not if we want to pursue well-being and happiness and remain true to ourselves.

As an illustration common to almost everyone in work, when we are writing our cv or resume, there is no need to include failures (unless they are glorious ones) but there is also no need to worry about what we will say if asked about them. Just agree they happened, that we have diagnosed the cause and we are confident they will not happen again because we have taken actions X and Y, and move on.

Storm off Brisbane, at the end of Pacific Crossing
2006

19. Importance – What grabs our attention? Fashionable decisions

> It was difficult to ignore the sharks. I can't say I was ecstatic about diving down with the sharks still in the vicinity, but someone had to; I focused hard on the anchor that was stuck in the coral and tried not to think about the sharks.

Suppose we are ill and aching, and someone asks how happy we were 10 years ago? The likelihood is that we would think of some events from about 10 years ago, and then examine them from the point of view of what is most significant to us now. This is likely to include a lot of attention to aches and pains and we might well conclude that we were much happier then than now. This may be why older people often remember their younger days as 'the happiest days of their life' – because they naturally focus on the aspects of their current life that comes to their attention most – like aches, restricted mobility, failing memory, less energy etc. And they don't think about the negative aspects of being young, like having less money, rejections by girl or boy friends, interviews, exams, etc because these are not so important to them now.

Similarly, if we are in the middle of commuting to work or in some dismal airport lounge, or at work struggling against some deadline and we think about the alternatives, we may well think longingly about those alternatives which do not involve interrupted journeys, stressful work etc. because those features are particularly important to us now. We will probably overlook other aspects that do not come to mind so easily – maybe lower income, less support, lower status etc.

So ideally if we were making decisions about what we will do in the future, we should spend time investigating what aspects are important to people in similar situations to those that we are considering – rather than just thinking about the things that occur to us now – like our awful boss and the long commute to work, and the stress of deadlines. That is not to say that these are not relevant, but they will not be the only factors that will influence whether we are likely to be happy in a new situation in the future.

Nudging us to make the right decision

But the plain fact is that we are often not very good at making the big decisions in our life – we really are swayed by our momentary mood or by external influences such as what we think others want us to do (we might call this fashion). This is not trivial. To take an example, when people are joining a firm, they are often given the chance to join the pension scheme, often one funded generously by the employer. (See Appendix 1 for why they may do this). One might think that this is a no-brainer, it makes sense to join. And so people do – when this is presented as the default case. The presumption is that they will join, but they have the chance to opt out.

But if the choice is presented the other way, the default is not to join, then most people do not join. The financial facts are the same in each case, the importance of the decision is clear, yet people are swayed by the importance of what they 'ought' to do, what is 'usual' to do. This is decision making by fashion or being nudged in the right direction, rather than by thought. It has parallels with the 'irrational exuberance' of bubble stock markets or property booms or any of the numerous mis-selling scandals. Another example is the cash back voucher given for example on computers where the purchaser can claim back an amount which makes the product attractively priced. Purchasers reduce the price by this amount when making comparisons, but in practice only about half ever get around to returning the voucher, which has lost its importance once the product is home. Expensive lawyers and advertisers are paid to persuade us that something is important when we might not have thought this before.

What is most important?

American executives regard income as much more important than vacations (holidays). When there are inequalities of pay, they are seriously concerned, but differences in vacation seem to matter much less. Whereas the French until recently paid more attention to time off and opportunities to be with their family and friends. These different sets of values will affect what grabs our attention in any given situation, and may explain why Americans tend to have 2-3 weeks' vacation as opposed to 5+ weeks in France.

We vary in what we regard as important. For example, when we are considering the recent past, we are likely to focus on actions we took that we now regret; whereas if we consider the more distant past, we are more likely to focus on actions we did NOT take. Which we focus on is more likely to influence our work and life decisions about the future.

We also need to be aware of the influence of advertisements and other marketing which try to persuade us to focus on those factors possessed by the products or services they are selling (like the size of a house, the speed of a car, or the status of the restaurant), and not towards other factors which may actually have more influence on our happiness (like how far away the house is from our friends and family, how reliable the car is, and the taste of the food and who we have the meal with). Spending on advertising amounts to more than 2% of total production which indicates how much we are influenced by it.

Therefore, there are attempts to ensure advertising is truthful and not misleading. In theory this should also benefit advertisers because even a few untruthful advertisements lead to a general feeling of cynicism and disbelief, in the same way that publicity on a few corrupt politicians leads to a belief that no politician can be trusted. In practice the oversight of advertisements leads to a variety of advertising stratagems, mostly stimulating desire, and suggesting consequences without ever actually promising them – like the lady draped over a car.

The investment to persuade us to buy goes far beyond this. The sales force in shops, salesmen going around businesses, market development executives using customer relationship marketing (crm) to develop relationships with the decision makers in potential client firms, are just a few examples of a mammoth sector of commerce. The spending on personal selling was more than double the spending on advertisements and is more than that now. Sales workers in 2000 made up 12% of total employment. So there are lots of people trying to persuade us to make decisions in ways that favour them. Japanese scientists are even measuring the perfect way to smile, as smiling stimulates liking and buying behaviour.

This increasing importance of relationships is a trend which includes access to celebrity parties for the rich, agents offering access to decision makers for a fee, head-hunters who cultivate connections, and social networking like Facebook which is likely to be a gold mine for those who 'sell their connections'.

It has been found that consumers typically only use a tiny fraction of the information available, or to consult when making major purchasing decisions. For example, only 1/3 of people checked with their partner before making major purchases of appliances. If people reach cognitive overload, (too much information to process) then decisions are typically made in a very simplistic way. For example, 'I'll have the biggest one' or the tactic beloved of advertisers 'I'll have that one because at least I recognise the brand' The importance of this when we are deciding what to do with our work and life is obvious.

Advertisements

Novelty, variety and promises of status persuade us to consume everything from yachts to cars to clothes. When food is usually the same, people eat less than when the food is varied. Certain people (the early adopters) actively seek out the latest product, idea or technique, and the rest of us follow on later, the take up rate depending on how 'must have' the item becomes, and availability of credit. TV programmes have ever shorter sequences, often only 1 second, to avoid us habituating, and constantly test the boundaries of what will really shock us. Advertisements have to be clever enough to entice us into their world, so are increasingly subtle and humorous, the exact mix varying in different countries and cultures – UK likes humour for example.

If you think you are immune to advertisements, just see how advertisements are tuned to each national culture, and increasingly are being aimed at even smaller groups right down to the individual. The styles shown below are obviously generalizations, but think of the styles you like yourself and which grab your attention. Check the advertisements when you visit these countries, or view an advertisement from a company from that country. I suspect you will find them close the mark. Essentially marketing exploits our weaknesses to persuade us to purchase, just as sportsmen analyse their opponent's weaknesses in order to win.

If we feel they have connected with us, it is usually because they have analysed the things we normally connect with and regard as important, and designed the approach accordingly. Social media give organisations massive evidence on what we value, enabling them to make 'suggestions' on what to buy based on our own preferences.

Culture	Typical Effective Advertising Style
American	Direct competitive approach, often in lesson form and personalized eg You...
British	Humour, and promise that if you buy you will stand out from the crowd. Focus on young people
German	Strong information orientation and explicit wording to avoid ambiguity.
Italian	Conceptual thinking, design, drama and theatre, respect for elders
Spanish	Uses visual metaphors, less direct than N Europe. Few celebrity endorsements
French	Theatrical and bizarre. Few lectures, much joie de vivre.
Dutch	Focus on thrift, modesty, 'comfort', humour, disrespect for authority
Swedish	Men are shown doing household chores, focus on companionship
Japanese	Apologise for intruding, tell a story, few facts, serene mood creating symbols

Based on: Global Marketing and Advertising Understanding Cultural Paradoxes – M de Mooij.

Fashion in clothes and design in cars and similar equipment is explicitly intended to stimulate desire through novelty and implicit status, making last year's fashion worthless or worse, while brand is intended to limit the overload likely to result, and to encourage loyalty, as are loyalty points, as well as providing the means to target each of us as an individual.

In the 1950's American car designs became ever more extreme in an attempt to persuade people to buy. An equivalent in evolution may be peacock tails – worse than useless in terms of function, but attention grabbing and yielding sexual and status benefits. So what is marketed to us is not necessarily what is best fitted to our real needs. Peacocks who were very good at foraging and providing food and shelter may have lost out to showy competitors with glamorous tail feathers. It is not always the fittest that survive. Americans realised this in the late 1950's when a wave of cheap imported cars like the VW Beetle which did not change design every year but got you from A to B cheaply and reliably started to become 'cool'.

Making decisions in aroused or cool mode

We need to remind ourselves of the difference between making decisions or imagining the future in an 'aroused' situation as compared to an unemotional or 'cool' situation. When they are considering the future in a cool or unemotional way, people frequently over-estimate their powers of resistance when they are in an aroused mood. So for example, people over-estimate their ability to resist a cigarette when they have given up smoking, or a drink when they are in a bar or pub. They can resist when they are in a 'cool' state, but when they are in an aroused state (which for smoking is frequently early in the morning) they change their mind. Similarly, for drugs, drinking and sexual arousal. Some of the evidence on this comes from studies covering such behaviours as date rape, and drug taking etc. Indeed, legislation dealing with a number of important decisions eg investments, time share purchases etc allows for a 'cooling-off period' precisely because we may well come to different conclusions in the cold light of day compared to when we are aroused, and are most easily influenced. Crowd leaders have long used emotion to arouse mob action and often violence, by focusing on the importance of some insult or injustice.

In summary when we are trying to make important decisions about our life, including whether to change job or to stop work, we need to be rigorous in determining what factors are likely to be really important in practice e.g. by asking others who have taken similar decisions before, or by talking to unbiased professionals. This is to counteract the perceived importance of some factors that spring to mind because of our present mood, or are promoted by marketing. We also should try to be unemotional, or at least to be aware of the effect on decision making of being in an 'aroused' state.

That's the 'ideal' – but we should also be aware that although we may strive to make decisions based on a clear thinking approach, in practice all too often we take decisions on a 'gut feel' or overall subjective feeling, and maybe deep down we believe that is the right thing to do. If so, this may be another example of our mind misleading us.

But there is one concern that we may already be considering. Is it possible that focusing on happiness is actually going to have a negative effect – make us unhappy? This is an important concern and is explored in the next chapter.

Elaine and Denis on Intrepid, Huahine, Pacific Ocean
2005

20. Happychondria. Does Focusing on Happiness really make us happier?

> Gauguin was looking for a way of life 'sauvage' – instead he found missionaries and governors who really did not want him, and in the end Gauguin died alone in the Marquesas in the Pacific, and his rough red stone grave still looks out over the bay.

We may question the very approach of deciding what to do with our work and lives on the basis of how happy we will be. The pursuit of happiness is a fundamental part of the Declaration of Independence, but this does not mean it applies to everyone; and we may be suspicious of the increasing focus of the media and indeed individuals on their own happiness. Indeed, we seem to be continually exhorted to 'be happy' or 'have a nice day'.

However, is this actually going to make us happier, and anyway is it the right thing to focus on ourselves anyway? Rightly or wrongly people are focusing on their own happiness, and are interested in anything that will help them to do this. Aren't we being a bit 'happycritical', shouldn't we focus instead on other people's happiness, or the well-being of society in general? Isn't a core skill to avoid being self-centred?

Focusing on happiness may also remind us of unhappiness - and this is particularly likely if we are currently feeling unhappy – just like the ill person tends to focus on aches and pains when considering what is important. If so, then focusing on happiness and changes that we think may make us happier, may simply exaggerate our current unhappiness and lead us to make decisions that do not make us any happier at all – may indeed make us unhappier still.

So for example, if we are currently unhappy in our marriage, or about being single (and everyone is unhappy in their marriage at some time, or is unhappy about being single), then if we focus on happiness, what is likely to happen is that we will make ourselves even more unhappy because of the contrast between what we are at the moment, and what we remember about the past or how we imagine others are. This is particularly likely if we are relatively high on the neurotic anxious worried personality scale, (which indicates we are more likely to respond quickly to negative events and situations). So in this case, we may decide that we are clearly unhappy, and may either decide to divorce or separate or become hyper anxious, if for example we decide the cause is external (our spouse or partner) and general (they are not going to improve). Or we may explain to ourselves that the cause is ourselves (internal) and general (I will never improve) and become depressed.

In both of these cases, a focus on happiness is likely to have exactly the opposite effect to that intended – we may become a happychondriac. As soon as we tell ourselves to NOT think about something, we inevitably think about it. That is why goals are best expressed as positives. So the people who say the best way to be happy is not to try to be happy but rather to get clear on our purpose in life, and happiness will come as a by- product may well be right. This is especially so if they are extraverts who as we have seen are likely to be particularly open to positive events in life, and respond to them quickly. But then they are likely to be happy anyway.

By contrast, people who are self-focused are unlikely to benefit much from focusing on their own happiness; they are less likely to have many friends and are more likely to become depressed, and focusing on happiness is likely to make the contrast even worse. Just as in business, an organisation that focuses completely on maximizing profits especially in the short term, is unlikely to make most profits longer term, so a person who focuses on achieving happiness in the short term is unlikely to do so in the longer term (and probably not in the short term either).

For people high on the anxious, worried neurotic scale, it may be better to avoid a focus on happiness, and instead to focus on being more relaxed and outgoing. We may prefer the term contentment or well-being rather than happy anyway. This is not going to be easy, but may include re-looking at our own values, looking for contentment and relationships, rather than achieving high visibility status goals; reducing change where practical and arranging long term situations where there is a relative absence of threatening or otherwise negative events; minimizing the possible impact of these; and strengthening our ability to cope with them. Some of this may be achieved by analysing the causes of the negative events we react to, and insuring or otherwise working to avoid or reduce their effect. We may do this by reminding ourselves that we always have enough money to cover most situations, and are well insured. For example if our car is damaged, or our health deteriorates, we have enough money to overcome this quickly and without excessive worry; and even looking to have a new group of friends (maybe a new activity or club or class) so we have strength in depth in relationships.

Of course there is a down side to this risk avoidance. Remember that one of the greatest causes of happiness is being with family and friends? Well, one of the ways to avoid being hurt by relationships is to avoid them, or at least to keep them safe, and 'at a distance'. But this means that we will often lose out on the positive benefits of relationships which is likely to mean that our happiness is lower than it might otherwise be. Whoever said that being happy is easy?

Well, actually it may be for extraverts, because their genetic makeup leads them naturally to explore and jump into lots of possible positive happy experiences. Some of these may turn out to be not so good after all, and there is a price to be paid in terms not just of emotional well-being, but also physical well-being. There is evidence that extraverts have more accidents, and are more likely to be badly injured or die young than introverts. And we may surmise that because they start more relationships, they are likely to have more relationship breakdowns – and indeed there is evidence that extraverts have a higher divorce rate for example than introverts.

Since our personality is relatively fixed, it may not pay to dwell on changing our personality for too long, since there are advantages and disadvantages to most types of personality, although as already mentioned on average extraverts report being happier than introverts, and stable personalities happier than neurotics. This may well be due to extraverts engaging in more activities that are attractive and exciting, so the chances are that when they are asked about their happiness they are actually involved in just such an activity, or have just finished it, and so report increased happiness.

But in the end, we are more likely to be happier if we know what makes us happier, even if we do not focus on this. So in Part 3 we examine what we can do about changing our working life to give ourselves the best chance of being happy and creating happiness for those who matter to us. Because that is what we really want to do.

Intrepid of Dover in mid Pacific

Part Three:

How to live a happier, more contented life?

21. HOW CAN WE USE THIS KNOWLEDGE IN PRACTICE?

> We take comfort from other accounts of sleepless nights as squalls hit the boats, or discuss ways round calm patches 100's of miles wide, but in the end we are together alone, 1500 miles from anywhere....

Our reaction to what has gone before in Parts 1 and 2 may be confusion – so many factors, all interlinked, many of the most important factors outside our control, (how do I change my personality, or get a more satisfying job paying more? Or even get married to someone I love – if I don't know who this is?) And in any case, general advice is too general – how do I know whether this is the right person to marry, or whether this job is right for me, or whether I should stop work? We are usually faced with real specific decisions to make, and there is quite enough advice around without adding more complications. So should we just forget about happiness and get on with living?

Well, it's certainly one approach, and if we are of a free and easy nature, in a reasonably well paying job, (or access to income in some other way) then this should work fine. But for most of us, it's a bit like saying we can ignore modern knowledge, and for example continuing to smoke or not exercise when the knowledge is available that ignoring this is likely to make us ill sooner or later.

Of course we can, and people until recently had to, but given that all this information about happiness is now available, it seems a shame to ignore it. And it's not as if the pursuit of happiness is a new target – as we saw, it was around at the time of the American Declaration of Independence in 1776 and the concept is a lot older. So what we need is a way to use the knowledge without becoming so self-focused that we end up unhappier. Just like TV for example, we need to learn how to use it to entertain us, without it coming to dominate our life, and end up being deadly bored because we can't think what else to do.

People have been searching for this elusive secret for years – all the self-help books and religions and philosophers can reasonably claim they are there to help us find the way to true happiness – usually defined the way they want it defined. And we can read the books or listen to the programs or attend the services and sometimes be inspired by some passages. However, we may also feel at times that it may work for 'them', but we are different and we want something that really works for us that is tailor made, because we are unique.

Politicians also search after happiness, because they suspect (probably correctly) that if only they can make the majority of voters happy (or less unhappy) then the voters are likely to vote for them again. So it is strange that with a few exceptions (like Bhuttan), no politician says that their goal is to make people happier. Perhaps the politicians are put off by the thought that if decades of greater prosperity have not made people in the developed countries any happier, then this may be something best avoided at least in targets, and get on with something simpler like GDP growth, national health, job creation and nuclear deterrence which (they think) they know how to deliver.

But to come back to our feeling of being unique. We are – in a way. But because psychologists have been trying to categorize us to a greater or lesser extent, even though each individual is genuinely unique (even identical twins have different experiences though they may have the same genes), it is still possible to make predictions, based on who we are.

The starting point for any pursuit of happiness is to know ourselves. Not in a navel gazing internally focused even obsessive way, but just describing and realizing the sort of person we are. We need to do this for all sorts of reasons. Indeed, even leaving happiness aside, we need to be aware of the sort of person we are, our skills and weaknesses, our ambitions. We do this when deciding what job or career we want to follow, and before that which subjects to study at school or University, and during all this what sort of people we want to be friends with. This includes the idea of making others happy. It's complex enough as it is, and if we think of many well-meaning but misguided attempts (including politicians) there is no guarantee that this will do any good. Indeed, trying to make someone else happy without being very clear about our own goals, feelings, values, etc is likely to do more harm than good.

Planning ahead

At age 40 we have had 15-20 years of challenging, pushing, putting maximum effort into our business life, our family life, our sports and leisure life, testing ourselves against others in everything from promotions, income, houses, cars, children, attractiveness and sexual ability. We have often been preoccupied with accumulating wealth, presenting our best front to the world, we have worried extensively about how we appear to others, and working out how to please others and to get bonuses or approval in general. We anxiously look for feedback from those in power. We have a strong sense of competition on those things we value.

As we live longer, the time we have to plan for after we stop working for an organisation is now realistically 25 -30 years or more. Up to age about 70 we have a reasonable expectation of remaining physically in good shape, although reduced muscle tone etc will start to require major exercise from age 55 or so if it is not to affect our ability to perform strength and agility based tasks. After age 70, we may well start to focus on avoiding bad things rather than looking for good things, and we have to be concerned at the need for long term care – which is partly why having an investment in property appeals to many – either we stay in it rent free, or we can sell it at the time we move into long term care and use the money to pay for the care.

In other words, our planning for a change of job needs to take a 30 year plus timescale – not easy, particularly if we think back to when we started work. If we think of the situation when we started work compared to now, and the significant events that affected our lives, it is clear that there is a great deal that is out of our control, ranging from war and peace, crime, global warming, inflation, stock market crashes or booms, technology advances like medicine transport and communication, population change (the aging population in Europe for example), political change (like the EU), taxation, plus of course our own health and circumstances including those of our family and people dependant on us. The list is so long it is tempting to do nothing – but doing nothing is just as 'risky'.

The need is to develop a plan that recognises some of the possible scenarios, and alter our plans until they are reasonably robust to many of the events we may foresee. Wealth is one of the robust ways in which we can shield ourselves in the future – but like any insurance, it is possible to pay too much for insurance or try to insure against everything, and end up unable to accept any risk, and achieve nothing. Interestingly, low income earners seem to take more risks than higher income earners – but also have more accidents. The trick is to know when to stop focusing on insurance or avoiding risk, and get on with enjoying our life – happiness in fact

So that dream may well be more possible than we think. It's a matter of budgeting for it and re-focusing on what we really want and what we are just doing out of habit or laziness – just like a spending review in a business aims to re-prioritise spending onto those activities that are essential for the strategic goals, and strips away those that are nice to have.

This combination of knowledge of what makes us happy and how we can be misled, will give us the self-confidence to get out and pursue our dreams, rather than worrying about what might happen.

We need to think in terms of:

1. Things we are unlikely to be able to change, and we had better get used to; and
2. Things that if we want to, we could have a reasonable chance of changing

Based on the all the Chapters in Parts 1 and 2, here is a Summary that describes all the factors that are likely to influence our happiness, an approximation of their effect, and how easy it is to change them by ourselves:

Factors affecting happiness and likelihood of changing them.

Situation or Change	Approximate Influence on Happiness	How easily we can make this happen	Comment
Increase in income of 30%	+3%	Medium – we can work harder, but we may not earn more; we can apply for a higher paying job – but may not get it.	After one year, 'required income' has risen by 40% of the increase, so happiness is reduced. If extra work is required, may be negative.
Family income goes down by 1/3 in real terms (but is still more than £18,000/$24,000/person)	- 3%	Medium	Voluntary downsizing, may be positive because of reduced stress
Reduction in family income to less than £18,000/$24,000/person.	- 10% or more; chance of depression	Medium – in a developed country, we may keep income above £18,000/$24,000/year.	Government has a role here, eg benefits.
Reduction of Income relative to people we compare with (eg they get a raise and we don't)	- 4%	Medium – even working longer hours is unlikely to help.	If we downsize, there may be other effects eg less stress
Made unemployed	- 6%	Low. It can happen to anyone from CEO down.	May cause depression or be seen as an opportunity to change direction.

Situation or Change	Approximate Influence on Happiness	How easily we can make this happen	Comment
Insecure job	- 3%	Medium. We can choose secure jobs (sometimes lower paid) or risky ones.	May be a payoff with income
Being in work but unemployment rate goes up by 10%	- 3%	Zero.	Presumably causing insecurity
Loss of Personal Freedom or Control in what we do, eg increasing Government control or loss of discretion at work or elsewhere	- 10% to - 30%	In our job and family and leisure life, we have some influence on our personal control, but a new boss or policy may reduce our personal control.	Depends on how we explain events; our perception may be more important than actual level of control.
Other work factors	Varies	High. The problem is knowing what sort of things make us happy, and then finding a job that provides this. Will change over our career.	Chapter 5.
Getting married	+ 4 to + 6%	Medium. Most people can marry someone – but is it a 'suitable' person?	A happy marriage has a big effect – but how do we know who to marry (and will they marry us?)
Cohabiting not married	+ 2 to + 3%	Low-Medium.	Compared to being single.

Situation or Change	Approximate Influence on Happiness	How easily we can make this happen	Comment
Separated during marriage	- 8%	Medium – it depends on the relationship and how hard we will both fight to keep it intact.	Initial unhappiness may later lead to an increase.
Widowed	- 4%	Low or zero.	Marriage increases longevity
Divorced (rather than married)	- 5%	As for separation.	
Having Children	0 (after 2 years)	High. We can usually choose whether to have children.	After initial burst of happiness, and later when children leave home!
Having parents who separate or divorce	Significant negative effect	Low or zero.	2x possibility of being depressed, or suspended from school, 7 x chance of imprisonment, on average may live 4 years less
Moving to a community where we feel people can't be trusted or the community we are in changing	- 1% to -2%	High. We can choose where we live, although other factors eg work, school will limit or influence this.	This could be really the case, or just our perception.

Situation or Change	Approximate Influence on Happiness	How easily we can make this happen	Comment
Ill health (down 1 point on a 5-point scale or '20% less healthy')	- 6%	Low-Medium. We can take some steps to keep ourselves healthy but there are no guarantees. People adapt to long term ill health	Happy people are more likely to be healthier, so it works both ways.
Being a member of a religion	+ 3%	High. We can usually choose to join on not.	May be due to social interaction; joining a club is an alternative.
Neurotic, anxious, worried Personality	- 6% to -28% Significant	Low. We can influence our personality to some limited extent – self help books, NLP, professional help, medicines.	However, this personality is likely to spot problems early, and is therefore valuable.
Extrovert outgoing, sociable Personality	+2 to +16% Significant	As above.	Also increases chance of other positive events
Other Personality Factors Especially Openness to Experience	+ 2 to +14%	As above.	Mainly quicker adaptation.
Higher Social Class	+ 4%	Medium- we can to some extent choose our profession, but we may be limited by our ability and resources.	We may be 'born' into a particular social class, but there is some mobility.

Situation or Change	Approximate Influence on Happiness	How easily we can make this happen	Comment
Getting Older	+ 1%	Zero. We may think we are younger than we look but we are just kidding ourselves.	Women have lowest average happiness at 37, men at 42; after this the future is brighter!
Male (rather than Female)	+ 1%	Zero. Transgender change excluded.	Women tend to blame themselves for failures and generalise this
Having a materialistic set of values which rates <High income, job success and prestige>; higher than <having close friends and a close marriage or family partnership>	- 5%	Medium. Our values initially come from our parents and friends- but we also influence them partly by making them explicit.	Placing a high value on friends and family to makes people happier; focus on 'success and status' makes us unhappier.
'Bored' eg watching too much poor TV	Negative, and likely to be Significant	High- but it needs us to identify alternatives and do them.	People who garden or go to theatre are happier than watching TV
Exercise, Dance Sport or similar	Up to +20% Significant	High. The environment we live in may encourage us or not.	3 periods of exercise/week over 6 months

Siuation or Change	Approximate Influence on Happiness	How easily we can make this happen	Comment
Getting 'in the flow' ie getting so involved in the activity we are doing that we lose all sense of time.	Significant Positive	Medium; Depends on whether our job and/or leisure activity gives us lots of chances to 'get in the flow', but we can choose these activities.	We are unlikely to get 'in flow' for more than 1-2% of our time, but when we do the effect is great.
Intelligence and Education	Low or zero	Medium. We can do little to increase our intelligence, although using our minds even in old age retains mental ability. Education is always possible.	Education may give greater income, health & self-control, but also a more demanding reference group, and awareness of risks & threats

So in summary, what factors that cause happiness can we influence? We would like to find lots of causes that have a big effect, and we can easily influence, but that is not the case. There are a few, some surprising, but many of the others we have to work hard at. The table below summarises these. Causes that are likely to result in an increase in happiness are marked with a (+), those that cause a reduction in happiness (and we would therefore like to reduce or eliminate) are marked with a (-).

Effect on Happiness	Easy to change	Possible to change but not easy	Difficult to change
Big Effect 8%+	1. Sport, Dance, Other Activities (+) 2.Avoiding being 'Bored' (eg being active, not watching lots of TV) (+);	1. Avoid Household income dropping below £18,000/person (+); 2. Being made unemployed (-); 3. Personal Control and how we explain events (eg one-off, bad luck for negative events; and influenced by me for good events) (+); 4. Paying attention to events we can influence not those we can't (+); 5. Getting in 'flow';	1. Having or developing a stable, easy going Personality (+); 2. Having an extravert outgoing Personality (not self-centred) (+).
Medium Effect 4-7%	1. Separating during marriage (-)	1. Decrease in income but still above £18,000/$24,000/ person (-); Increase in income relative to the people we compare ourselves with (+); 2. Getting married (+); 3. Divorcing (-); 4. Keeping Healthy (+); 5. Moving to a Higher Social Class (l); 6. Having Values that favour family and friends rather than status (+).	1. Being in a secure (rather than insecure) job (+); 2. Widowed (-); 3. Having parents who separated (-); 4. Ill Health (-); 5. Agreeable, (+) conscientious, (+) open to experience (+) Personality

Effect on Happiness	Easy to change	Possible to change but not easy	Difficult to change
Low Effect 3% or less	1. Having children (+); 2. Becoming a member of a Religion (+).	1. Increasing income (+); 2. Cohabiting (+); 3. Moving to an area where you feel you can trust people more (+). 4.Better Education (+)	1. Unemployment rate up by 10% (-); 1. Getting older (after 39-42) (+) 3. Male (+). 4. Intelligence

This table, while still a generalization does start to indicate where we can most usefully focus our attention. But this depends on getting clear what we really want to do. This is covered in the next Chapter.

Arrival Marquesas after 28 days at sea, 3000 miles from Galapagos

22. Clarifying our Goals

Now we are aware of the factors in the Table in the previous Chapter, it's worth doing a number of exercises to work out what we really want to do, starting with writing down or imagining in as vivid a way as we can what we think we want, then asking Why?

Write down the answer to that Why? and then ask Why? Again, and keep going until we realize 'There isn't a Why? that's just what I want to do.' Psychology has some things to say about this approach, but probably more important is honesty and a quiet feeling that we have the right to say what we want, and it is going to help us and those around us if we are clearer on what that is.

It doesn't mean that what we want to do has to be selfish or self-centred. It may well be to help people or to create something for the enjoyment of people, but what matters is that we are clear about what we want to do. It should be based on our 'signature skills' those skills we have that we feel most comfortable with, skills that help us get 'in the flow' and which in some senses define us. However, research indicates that people are only in 'flow' (when everything seems to be going right and we lose all sense of time) about 1% of the time. So other people focus more on a longer term sense of contentment, where it is not the peak or target that is desired, but rather a longer term sense of being in the right place at the right time and everything working.

Some people find it helps to create a collage of cuttings that represent their idea of what they want, different angles on the subject, some people like to talk things through with a friend or counsellor, or to write a personal mission statement that can be reformed and modified day by day until we are satisfied. The level of detail can be varied, for example does it make a difference when this happens, and there may be many different ways to achieve the same end, are all these acceptable? And what level of risk are we comfortable with?

What we want may well be multi-faceted – covering work, leisure, family, friends, any of the many roles of our life. But if we are being really honest with ourselves, we will probably find that one or two aspects dominate, without which we would regard our life as missing some crucial aspect. This need for clarity in what we want to do is of course key in deciding on a career, or a career change or whether to stop working, as well as all the other work and life decisions we have to take.

There are number of exercises that we can do by ourselves that are flexible and powerful to help define what we really want. Here is the most flexible one:

Underlying Motivators

Think of 3 activities or jobs or ways of living or targets that seem at first sight to be most appealing. These need to be as strong as you can, but don't worry too much about being absolutely precise about them – the exercise will bring this out. Call these 3 activities or jobs or ways of life A, B and C. (If we want a 4th and 5th that is fine, but we need at least 3).

Now think of at least 2 activities or jobs, or ways of life, or targets that are decidedly unappealing – that we really would not want to do, that we would avoid if possible, that we personally feel would not be right for us. If we have more than 2 that is fine, but we need at least 2. Call them X and Y.

We should now have the following table:

	Description
A Preferred Activity/Job/Target	....
B Preferred Activity/Job/Target	....
C Preferred Activity/Job/Target	....
X Disliked Activity/Job/Target	....
Y Disliked Activity/Job/Target	....

Now consider these in threes: 2 preferred and 1 disliked and ask 'What have the 2 liked activities/Jobs/Targets in common? And how do they differ from the disliked one?'

165

	Ways in which the 2 preferred are similar, and ways in which they are different from the disliked.
A, B, X	....
B, C, Y	....
A, C, X	....
B, C, X	....
A, C, Y	....

Examine the words we have written in the boxes above, and it will start to become pretty clear what are the common themes. Reduce these to between 3 and 5 'Underlying Motivators' by summarizing and finding the best words to express what are the crucial differences. These are our underlying motivators, and they benefit from being defined by ourselves, rather than by a standard psychometric measure.

Knowing our underlying motivators gives us a powerful insight into what is likely to give us the best chance of being happy or fulfilled or in the flow – in effect our goal or what we mean by contentment.

These motivators may change over time, and are affected by our current mood and what factors are especially important to us at the moment, but nonetheless this will go a long way to clarifying the sorts of things we want (or don't want). It's better to express these in terms of things we want, rather than things we don't want, but if the 'avoid' motivation is very powerful, then leave it as it is.

In my case, this exercise indicated to me that I wanted to get out of an office and go sailing oceans. It didn't need to be much more detailed than that, but I did need to be clear on the impact on others, and the resources I needed to do it. That's covered in the next Chapters.

Sunset Raiatea, Pacific Ocean,
2005

23. What do we really want to do; what lifestyle would really make us happy?

> But as the storm raged we finally were able get directions from a volunteer coastguard, and tied up at the rather unfriendly locked windy quarantine berth in Brisbane just before dark at 6pm, and opened the champagne because WE HAD SAILED ACROSS THE PACIFIC. 8000 miles. It's been one of the most enjoyable, instructive and challenging years of my life. Maybe the three go together.

The key to all this is to develop a clear sense of purpose of what we want to do. Remembering the distinction between active enjoyment and contentment, this does not necessarily have to be grand achievements. It may be having more time with our family and friends. But we do need to be clear on what we want. And this is not easy.

All too often we tend to think that what we would really like to do is impractical, requires too much resources, (usually money) or the cooperation of people like our partner that may not be forthcoming, so it gets shelved and we continue working and getting more and more frustrated because we are pursuing a goal that isn't what we really want at all. And of course just like a business that hasn't thought through its strategy, this ambivalence leads to mis-communication, loss of coherence and motivation, 'taking our eye off the ball', waste of time and resources and loss of confidence.

Many self-help books don't talk about money at all, but it is an important component. (Conversely, financial books don't usually cover self-reliance). However, money is unlikely to be critical. If the goal is clear, there may be many more ways to sort money than is apparent at first glance.

When planning our goal, it is important to have a realistic estimate of how much money it will require, because otherwise our escape to freedom may end up making us unhappier than before. And we need to have a reserve of money or skill or family back-up that we can call on if the worst happens, either by insurance or money in the bank or strong family ties. This sounds awfully pragmatic when we are planning an escape from it all, but it is necessary.

The positive side to this is that living our dream may not cost as much as we think at first. Part of the reason why income does not seem to have a very big effect on our happiness, is that we are often so over-worked, and so influenced by often subtle advertisements or inducements to buy something we hadn't realised we needed, that we are not very good at spending money effectively to achieve a purpose. This is particularly so if we have a surplus over what we need for genuine essentials. If our income is reduced, over time our need for money may unbelievably start to decrease.

There are a number of cases where a change of job or moving to a different way of life may even make money. For example, there are so many property development programmes on TV nowadays that the implication is that this is an easy way to make money. It isn't but at least a property usually holds more of its value over a longer period, whereas a car or boat or piece of furniture loses value. So if we are looking for an alternative life style, and money is a concern, then buying property or starting a business is a way forward.

Businesses that do not have a clear strategic view often start projects without the resources needed, where people don't have the tools to do the job, pursue divergent objectives, and the result is often serious loss and public humiliation. The strategic review that organisations use can work for us, but the main point can be stated very simply: Once we have worked out what we really want to do, we need to check the resources we need. We probably have all the resources we need, and if we haven't, we can get them, we just may need extra time. Even better we will enjoy getting them because we can see they are a means to an end, a REAL end that we have worked out for ourselves, and just this coherence will keep us going through any number of frustrating meetings or challenges.

Positive Goals Not Negative Goals

It's important to state our goal in a positive sense. There are some individuals whose main motivation is to avoid or stop doing some thing or activity, like 'stopping work'. Whilst it is very important to listen to the message implicit in this, it is more useful, practical and more likely to lead to action if the goal is stated in a positive sense. It is also best to state our goal with any conditions or difficulties to be overcome stated first, then the goal, rather than the other way around. We tend to focus on the peak and end of activities and even statements, so if we end our statements or goals with conditions or difficulties we will tend to focus on these and reduce the powerful motivational effect of a well stated goal. So for example, 'To raise the finance, learn the skills and then start a successful organic venture' is better than: 'To start a successful organic venture, provided I can raise the finance and learn the skills'.

Working out what we really want may well involve giving up an earlier goal, which we haven't achieved. This may seem like an admission of failure, or giving up. In fact, if approached well, it is exactly the reverse, as we saw in the chapter on failures. It seems that the most balanced, effective, even happy people are those who know when to give up on a goal without it affecting our own self esteem. And this stands to reason. After all, not everyone can be President or Prime Minister or CEO and while a few do, there are plenty of very fulfilled lives that do not involve this. Conversely for every person who does reach a particular position like CEO or President, there is a significant chance that their tenure will end in failure or disgrace, so as a goal it may have been a step too far for them. So knowing when to change goals and how, is important for our own self esteem. Everyone has to do it and it is only the fool who insists that they will never give up on a particular goal (unless the activity itself is satisfying even if the goal is not achieved).

A particularly insidious form of counter-productive target is the 'I need £x million to be truly happy and I have to keep working until I get there'. This is explored in more detail in the section on working out what money and other resources you really need for the life you want to lead, but a few words are in order here. Psychologists and economists have developed the idea of utility – that an extra £1000 means more to someone who has nothing, compared to someone who already has £1,000,000. It's the same amount of money yet the satisfaction and indeed the 'happiness' is likely to be greater for the person who starts with less.

We often have 2 resources in mind – money and time, and our choice of goals is likely to be determined by the best balance of happiness we can achieve between the two. We can ask ourselves 'How much is my time worth?' 'How much would we have to earn (after tax and so on) to be worth working over a weekend, or even over the next 5 years?'

There is no simple answer to this. It may depend whether the weekend is especially important, a birthday perhaps, or whether there is some special event (a big sporting event perhaps). Another factor will be how pleasurable is the work we are being asked to do, also how much money we already have or how much we think we 'need' (the latter is the utility issue).

At some point we may ask ourselves 'How much would I have to earn to be worth working for another year instead of doing what I really want to do? In other words, we will be comparing the happiness we gain from a year doing what we really want to do, compared to a year working and earning money. It's a trade-off between money and life satisfaction.

(Time and satisfaction at work + earnings less tax) -v- (Time and satisfaction doing what I really want + net income when doing this).

This is why it is so important to be clear on what we really want to do. If this is vague then the equation will be vague, and we may well continue doing the same thing and miss opportunities, and quite possibly (like businesses) end up in a difficult situation because the world around us has changed and so have we, and we haven't noticed it. So strategy is much like evolutionary change – it gives us a better chance. One of the best ways to do this is sabbaticals and working part time, in other words trying it out on a small scale first.

Money promised to us in the future has a lower value than money today (discounted cash flow or dcf). £100 now is more valuable than £100 in 5 years' time. We may use the same approach to time. So time this weekend or this year does actually have a greater value than time further in the future. So whilst it's advisable to plan for the long term, in the long term we are all dead, and no-one on their death bed ever said they wished they had spent more time at the office (to combine two truisms). We can use a system of discounted time flow (dtf) to remind us that time is also passing us by, the longer we put off doing what we really want to do. This is explored in a later Chapter.

We need a balance. Some of us are naturally thrifty, workaholics, who seem to prefer working or saving to fun and spending. Our satisfaction is money in the bank, or targets achieved. There is a reason that our society places such a high value on thrift and hard work and doing our duty. If this were not the case, then more of us would probably get up when we wanted, laze around, do a minimum of work, chat to our friends - we found this situation in some south Pacific Islands for example. We would probably be happy, but unlikely to make any progress on any of the threats facing us like disease, food shortage, natural disasters or even war. So actually our existence and our happiness and the happiness of those who depend on us would be quite fragile, vulnerable to all sorts of threat. We may even find that our happiness is spoiled by the realisation that other people have worked and saved and are now enjoying a higher standard of living (in the easily observable material things) than we are.

So some societies have explicitly developed values which place a high priority on discipline, hard work, saving for the future, helping those in need who will then help us when we need something. Cold winters have an especially vivid way of making these virtues obvious, and it may be why societies living closer to either pole have often developed these disciplines and internalized the values of hard work and saving. Max Weber called it the Protestant work ethic. And Victorian books regularly promote the idea of restraint, delay of gratification, not doing what we want now, but saving it for the future. It includes restraint on sexual behaviour, and rules on commitment (marriage) to provide a framework for sex without losing control. For example, Kinsey found that college graduates in the USA had later sexual initiation than others (by 5 years) and half of college students were still virgins.

Whether this discipline is genuinely genetic, or just learned from birth in nursery tales onwards we don't yet know. But certainly this discipline is a very important part of the value system of many people, particularly of the professional, higher income earners, and education and income do seem to give an advantage in this respect. Delay of gratification does give people an increased chance of a better financial future. So this is self-reinforcing through generations – wealth provides education, sexual restraint, and income which together reinforce discipline which in turn promotes more education income and wealth.

The problem is that it can also turn us into misers, who die unhappy and unfulfilled millionaires. Or a driven man (or woman) who is so obsessed by the need to achieve that we lose all sense of perspective, and end up as failures emotionally and in a business sense because we antagonize all around us, and don't see the wider picture that a more relaxed, happier person might.

So just as a business can have a successful strategy or an unsuccessful strategy, so we can choose a successful personal strategy or an unsuccessful one.

Elaine Denis and Nicky en route Pago Pago – Suvarov, Pacific Ocean 2005

24. PERSONAL STRATEGY AND CHOICES ON THE WORK WE DO – SCOUTING THE FUTURE

> Christian and I untangled our fishing lines (again) while ripe bananas rained down on us from the complete hand of bananas we have tied on the back, and we hold (again) fishing strategy reviews that produce .... the same result (no landed fish) – they are simply too big for our tackle when they do strike, and on our only really heavy tackle they don't strike. No-one else caught anything either until Anaconda won our private wager and landed a 12 lb wahoo... and emailed us just to make sure we knew!

It makes sense to concentrate on the things we can change or at least influence, which also have a large or at least a medium effect on happiness. And to more or less ignore the items that we can't change or which only have a small effect (except where it is possible to insure against bad events we can't control).

Any decision to change job or stop work is likely to have a large effect on a number of the big hitting factors. Here is a checklist of some of the changes that a new job or life style may give us, some positive some negative:

* More chance for sport, activities, hobbies and even dance. (+)
* Greater boredom (watching TV etc) (-)
* Drop in income/person to below £18,000/$24,000person/year (-) which is likely to have significant adverse effects on happiness.
* A lowering of self esteem if we are made unemployed (-). However if we can persuade ourselves that we have taken the step ourselves, then this may even be a positive change (+).
* A change in personal control can give either an increase or decrease (+/-). This is really a matter of judgment – if we are in a job which gives us significant control over our activities and the activities of others, then if we lose this influence because of the change of job, we are likely to feel a significant drop in happiness (-) until

adaptation reduces this. On the other hand, if we feel we are already significantly controlled by or influenced by others, then moving to a different job or stopping altogether may actually increase (+) our sense of personal control. It's really a matter of what we can arrange for the next job, or what we will do if we stop work,

* Changing our mental view of the world ie what we pay attention to – if we focus on things that we can't control, (like the past, or events outside our influence) we are likely to be unhappy (-). However, if we focus on events we can influence, we are likely to feel happy (+).

* Moving to an environment (new organisation or community or country) where we feel freer to do what we want (+).

* Developing a mental view where we perceive most good things as caused by ourselves, and likely to continue, and most bad things to be one offs, and the result of bad luck (+).

* Giving ourselves the best chance of getting 'in flow' ie activities where we are so absorbed that we lose track of time in work or leisure (+).

* Developing an outlook on life which is stable rather than anxious or neurotic; and outgoing rather than self-centred and introverted. So not being a Happychondriac, (ie not focusing on our own happiness, because this is effectively being introverted) but rather seeking to enjoy the good things in life that occur (+).

* Trying to have an income relatively equal to or higher than our peers (ie our reference group – the people we compare ourselves with) (+). This can be achieved either by changing our reference group, or changing our (relative) income. We need to bear in mind that people in our reference group will also have changing incomes, and it may be easier to change our reference group than our income, provided we don't lose long term friends.

* Keeping healthy or at least as healthy as we can (+).

* Valuing family and friends over status. This is particularly relevant when changing jobs or stopping work – the perceived loss of status can be extreme, and if status is highly valued then the perceived loss of self-esteem will also be extreme (--). On the other hand, if there is a move to focus more on family and friends, then there is

likely to be more happiness even if apparent status is reduced (no cars, secretaries, expense accounts etc) (+). This effect is likely to be passed onto our children, so as well as passing on our genes and wealth (if we have it) we also pass on our sense of values and this has the opportunity to make our children happier (valuing friends) or unhappier (valuing status).

* Staying in or moving to a higher social class or occupation – which may be defined by profession or at least the people we associate with (+), provided we do not lose the value we place on friends; or we may find that stopping work reduces our perceived status, and that this matters to us a lot (-).

* Moving to a more secure job, or other work or even a guaranteed annuity, even if it has lower status and/or lower income can actually increase happiness (+) especially so if it enables us to get into 'flow' more often and/or to interact with friends more, do more activities, sport etc.

* Doing things that are closer to what we regard as our purpose in life – and if we are not clear about this, doing some exercises to help us get clearer. This is covered in the next Chapter.

Checking what may lie ahead

As we have seen many of our 'defence mechanisms' work by misleading us, so ideally we need to make big life changing decisions based on hard facts. With so many emotions, personalities and influences around this is almost impossible – we like to think that we are rational, but as we have seen our emotions and personality actually have an enormous influence on our judgments. However, just as the military may send a scout ahead to check the ground ahead, so we can use people who have already made some of these big decisions and are now experiencing the results in the cold light of day as 'scouts'. These could be people who have:

- Stopped working and bought a sailboat/farm/garden/2nd villa or whatever
- Downsized their work so they now work 2 days/week.
- Moved from their current home to another part of the country
- Downsized their house and moved into an apartment perhaps in the city

- Separated from their partner for a trial period.
- Moved in with their children or asked one of their children to move into their own home.
- Decided to move to a residence abroad
- Changed jobs so that they no longer travel a long distance to work, perhaps even work from home.

Now of course we may very reasonably say that 'But we are not the same as those people, so their concerns, values and their outlook is not going to be the same as ours. We are unique'.

But in practice, their experience of how the decision turned out is likely to be in many ways very similar to ours. Although we are all indubitably unique, we are all much more similar than we sometimes think. (If nothing else our genetic coding has far more in common with others than differences). So using the experience of others as a way of scouting the future makes a lot of sense – certainly to complement our own emotion packed thoughts about how we will feel after we have settled into the situation following our decision.

So we can in some senses get the best of all worlds, using the psychology of happiness to indicate what is important, while checking with other people who have already done what we are thinking of doing; and continuing to keep our self esteem high by our positive mental outlook and our management of our own memory and view of the world.

Here are 6 points that we used to guide our plans for sailing: (these are included here as a practical example as well as in the footnote):

1. Make sure that the dream we are proposing REALLY is our dream, what we really want. Then go for it and enjoy every opportunity there is.

2. Stay in touch with friends and family, and involve and bring them along as well in whatever ways we can

3. Make a budget and more or less stay within it. If it becomes apparent that to enjoy the opportunity means exceeding the budget, work out ways to get extra income or spend less (eg renting our house, doing more maintenance ourselves or doing part time work as we go). Don't let the budget run our life.

4. Be as self-reliant as we can – we have already seen the evidence that one of the most important factors for happiness is personal control, and this is likely to be one of the greatest challenges and learning opportunities.

5. Manage risk. By all means if the excitement means a degree of risk, weigh it up then go for it, but reduce risk where it adds nothing to the quality of life, and also where there are efficient ways to reduce it eg by good planning, contingencies, and insurance

6. Retain our roots - think about our return.

Villagers dancing, Vanuatu
2005

24. Our income, what income we need, and what would 5 years of doing what we really want cost?

> One of the sadder sights we came across was a man who had worked for years to buy his dream yacht – a large Oyster – and within a few weeks of getting it realised that he was no longer fit or able enough to skipper it himself. So he had to hire a skipper, who hadn't taken enough care of the yacht, and when we met them the yacht was out of the water in Portugal for repairs with the owner wondering why it had all come to this, hiring someone to damage his own boat...

If I had to highlight only one conclusion, it is that when we are deciding what we really want to do, what will make for a fulfilled satisfying life, money may well play only a limited part in it. Money will never be absent, but it has a huge tendency to distort our idea of reality, and therefore to distort our values, our targets and ambitions. (See Appendix 1 for a fuller description of this). If we crowd our life plans around with too many restrictions about money, and our need for it, we are likely to miss many of the opportunities that life offers us. Part of this is fuelled by the needs and interest of many of those who we come into contact with every day, including our own family and friends. And this can even be unconscious. Remember that when people get a pay rise, after just one year, their needs have risen by on average 40% of the increase. In other words, we are on a happiness treadmill, as income rises, our needs also increase so we have to work harder and harder to meet them. The overall effect is to dramatically increase our perceived demand for money, well above what we managed to live on and be happy when we were (for example) students.

All the businesses and professionals that we buy goods and services from have a huge vested interest in persuading us that we need the newest, latest, most fashionable, most advanced product or advice or whatever. Indeed, they have whole departments devoted to just that – creating a need where none existed before. Even our employers need to motivate us to work harder, pay even more attention to detail, and to carry even more responsibility for growing the profitable business. The highly respected economist JK Galbraith proposed that if it were not for advertising and 'status envy' then many rational executives would only work at their main job 2 or 3 days/week. Seen this way, our whole society and community relies on an artificially induced need to maintain the economic growth that is seen by politicians to be the way to win the next election.

Or to put it another way, many of our executives are actually being completely irrational, not to say short-sighted when it comes to their own lives and motivation. And what does that say about their ability to make coherent intelligent decisions about the businesses they are running which will have consequences for thousands more? To say nothing about the people in their immediate or extended family.

When looking to the future, it is helpful to divide it into the short/medium term; and the long term. The short/medium term is from 3 months to about 5 years. We can do things in this time frame without losing our touch with the market, our contacts, our skills. We have a return ticket if not by contract then by skills. We can enjoy ourselves.

By contrast the longer term is likely to extend until we die, so we need to consider all stages of life and health and ill health. This can nonetheless be quite encouraging, as whilst we will have some limits on our ability to do what we want, these are likely for most of the time to be much less than when we are at work. We need to estimate our likely need for income to cover a happy and fulfilling life probably without a paid work income. We may want to exclude our home even if we own it, if we propose to stay there long term. However, take all our other assets, and apply financial rules of thumb like the 5% income approximation.

Income needed and how to fund it

This suggests that if we need an annual income of £10,000/year when we stop full time work then we need about 20 times that money to provide it long term allowing for inflation, management costs and market growth, i.e. £200,000 So an income of £50,000/year requires £1 million. Some people use 4% withdrawal rather than 5% - it depends to some extent on how the market does in the first 5 years; if it is going down use 4% to retain enough value for when the upturn comes. If we consider care somewhere other than our home, (which is likely to cost more) then we can include at least part of the value of our home in the calculation. We may decide that our children don't need much of an inheritance since they will be making their own provision anyway, they are likely to be 60 by the time they inherit, and extra money from an inheritance is unlikely to improve their motivation (Warren Buffet holds this to be particularly true).

Tax should reduce significantly as our income and tax bracket reduces. This means that tax saving schemes that worked before won't be as effective. But there will be other tax saving approaches like putting most income to the lower tax rated partner, or becoming self-employed or setting up a small company to enable you to set some business costs against income. This is the province of the financial and tax advisor and is outside what this book aims to cover. However financial advice often starts with the question 'What income do you need?' as though this is the easy part, and all that follows (the financial and tax mechanisms) are the hard part for which a fee is due. You would say that if you are a financial advisor. However, since we know that income above a certain level is only likely to have a small positive effect on our happiness, a clearer picture on what income and other factors we genuinely need to make us happy are actually the most important part of the wider question.

But for now let's focus on the short/medium term. Suppose we get a bonus one year, or win the lottery or an inheritance or a lump sum payment. It's quite a large sum even after tax, and we have to decide what to do with it. We may just use it to pay off debts, and this would probably be smart. But supposing even after paying off debts there is something left over. Of course, we can just put it in the bank, or we can invest it for... sometime in the future when we think of something we want or need; or we can buy something with it now. What should we buy? Maybe a car, or TV, or improve our house, or take a vacation, or a 2nd house or cabin, or give some to our children, or give it to a charity, or time off work...

Presumably (like a business with an investment budget) we could consider each opportunity, weight the cost of each and try to imagine the benefits we would get from each, (even giving to charity would be because we felt that this would give us the best feeling – that we had done the right thing). Of course we may not be so analytical, we may just see that new car in the showroom, and decide to buy it without considering any other alternatives.

How much of our spending is necessary?

Conversely, we can examine our spending to see what we would not need to spend if we were to change our ideas a bit. Commuting costs, business attire, a status car or two, a remodelled kitchen, bathroom or even complete house, the extra wide screen TV, the exclusive gym or golf club, the personal trainer or golf coach, meals in expensive restaurants to celebrate birthday, those vacation breaks that are needed because of the stress, and because otherwise we don't get to see our partner or children, the costly tools or equipment that are bought, used a few times then left, the expensive Christmas presents to make up for not seeing our children or partner as much as we should, surgery to improve the way we look, even the ultra-expensive children's education, possibly the 2nd home that we have no time to use, the insurance for everything, not to mention credit card debts and interest ...

Not buying some of these things depends on having a different mind-set – a different strategy and different priorities. If small is beautiful, rather than the latest or newest or most fashionable, then this different mind-set will create real differences in our spending. There may even be an incentive in a reduced tax bill if our income drops by even a little.

To use a different analogy, suppose we are working for an organisation in which we have no sense of ownership – we just work there. We are likely to be indifferent to costs, except insofar as they are required of us by targets etc. But suppose now there is a management buy-out or similar. Suddenly we own a share of the business, and our future is inextricably linked with its success. All of a sudden we may well find that we look at costs with a new eye, a more penetrating analysis, and find that there are many things that we can just do without, or do with something else that is cheaper or do things in a better way.

When we have worked out what we really want to do, then we may well see that a number of the things we buy are not actually contributing towards this, and we can therefore do without them.

What is a year off worth?

Suppose the idea of having a year off work doing precisely what we have always wanted drifts into our consciousness? A one-year sabbatical perhaps. Or 5 years? How should we compare this with the other alternatives? Well, in a way it's similar to buying a car, and even more similar to a vacation.

The cost however is more complex and has more implications and will vary from person to person. We will presumably lose our paid income, but will pay less tax, particularly if we choose our time away carefully so that it covers 2 tax years, in both of which we reduce our marginal rate of tax. We may get some form of income from an early pension if that is possible or from investments. We may choose to rent our house if we own it, if our chosen lifestyle involves living somewhere else. We will have some ongoing commitments, but also some that will no longer apply.

One of the biggest issues is whether we intend or are able to return to work (the same work or different) after being away. This will depend on our employer, the job market, our own skills etc. That's why if it is possible, taking a sabbatical with at least some form of re-entry discussion even if not guaranteed is desirable. But we may also recognise that our skills will still be marketable, and by staying in touch with some of our colleagues, we can ease the return to work if that is what we want. I returned to work after seven years sailing at a higher salary than I left – but this is not guaranteed! Be aware that final salary pension schemes have an inbuilt penalty for changing schemes mid-career – this can easily cost more than £100,000. This is explored in more detail in Appendix 1.

For now, though, let's see what it might be like in a highly simplified scenario that involves 5 years' time off work, and a return to different work afterwards:

Income/Cost	Now	Time Off	After
Salary	£50,000	0	£40,000
Tax	-£15,000	-£5,000***	-£10,000
Income from Investments	£10,000	£10,000	£10,000
Work related costs (commuting etc)	-£5,000	0	-£5,000
Holiday/New life style costs	-£3,000*	-£5,000	-£3,000
Cost of present accommodation	-£10,000	0	-£10,000
Cost of new life style accommodation	£0	-£15,000**	£0
Rental Income from renting out house	£0	£15,000	£0
Food, transport, other living costs	-£20,000	-£15,000	-£20,000
Donations to Charity	-£1000	-£1000	-£1000
Total (Surplus/deficit)	+£6000	-£16,000	+£1000

*Vacation;
** Assumes a modest accommodation
*** On rent and investment income.

In other words, on these very simple assumptions, if we stop work for 5 years and are able to return to work after this time at a slightly lower income (perhaps part time or with some consultancy work) then we would need £80,000 to fund the 5 years' time off.

We will also have to consider lots of other issues – partner, family and dependants, health insurance, effect on any pension plan of the absence, housing, control of investments, cost of managing investments, exchange rate movements, cost of living in a new location (which can be much cheaper), loss of contacts, the probability of being able to re-enter work at the same or similar income, and what to do if we can't. We are entering the unknown, so will also need some contingency money. Insurance companies are often reluctant to provide cover for anything that seems unusual or involves 'abroad', so this needs investigation, and if insurance is not available, then contingencies worked out (which is usually quite practical).

Certainly it is not a good idea to sell our own house or apartment (if we own one) to buy (for example) a boat. The differential price movements and depreciation mean that it is quite likely that we will be unable to buy a similar house back, and living on a boat long term has its drawbacks – especially as we get older or our health starts to deteriorate. On the positive side, rearranging investments into a safe low management cost, tax effective indexed portfolio geared to our particular circumstances (in terms of shares, bonds and cash, PEP's ISA's, Personal Pension Plans, and other tax effective investments) can often reduce management costs significantly (to 0.5%) and produce a better return, because there is not an annual drain of 2-3% management or trading fees, which on investments of £300,000 would be up to £9,000/year.

The figures will be very different for everyone. But the question on our very simplified figures, is whether 5 years of doing what we really want to, is worth £80,000? Put one way, this is only about 1.5 years' salary, for 5 years of doing what we really want to do, and for which the window of opportunity is now or at least the next few years. And what else can we spend the money on, because economists would say that this is really the only way to measure the value of anything?

We could presumably buy a car, a very small apartment, give it to charity, in fact all the things considered earlier. We could consult a financial advisor, who may confirm that very approximately a capital sum will provide $1/20^{th}$ (5%) as an annual income after retirement (some cautious people use 4% instead of 5%). Using 5%, £80,000 should provide an extra income of a bit less than £4000/year during all the years of retirement. So if we can decide on the basis of our memory of the past and our present mood and feelings and thoughts about the future, what will make us most happy £4000 extra/year; or 5 years of doing what we really want now; or buying something for £80,000?

And we might conclude that another car would just get us from A to B a few seconds faster and in marginally greater comfort, that our friends already have such a car, so there is no 'status' to acquiring it, that we can only live in one place at a time, so an apartment is only extra complexity, that we already give what we regard as a reasonable amount to charity already, and that just investing the money is only putting off a decision on what to do with it, when what we really want to do is... to do exactly what we want now, and not put it off.

So there are several parts to this debate – in effect, how much of our income do we really need, and how much is actually pretty marginal, where we know that we don't get much pleasure from spending it, even if we spend it at all? We may also find that after years of increasing demand for money, our need for money suddenly starts to reduce if we let it, as our mortgage comes close to being paid off, and any children we have start work and become financially independent (although don't bank on it!). We know that advertising and marketing, and competition with our reference group will all encourage us to spend all we can, and increase each year the amount that we regard as 'essential', but we can question this.

Some of this extra 'need' is technology progression, (it doesn't make much sense to try to retain an analogue or even black and white TV when digital is the standard), but another part of it is just 'froth' and probably increasing our carbon footprint into the bargain.

But we also know that if we change our reference group without losing our real friends, and stop focusing on what advertisers and marketing people and our present reference group want us to focus on, (like cars, TV's, houses, 2nd houses, vacations, fine food and wine, entertainment etc), and instead focus on what we really want, then our need for income will be much less. So we should end up with a more satisfying life, without running into debt. Because that is what we have been trying to do for years.

Is time now worth more than time in the future?

Discounted Time Flow

We may also think of the idea of discounted time flow – the idea that time now to do things we really want to do is worth more than the same length of time in the future. The traditional way of thinking about retirement was to work until aged 65 or so, then stop. But maybe this makes no more sense than waiting until we have all the money to buy a house, or start a business? If we followed this rule (admirable though it sounds) then we would be unlikely to buy a house until well into our middle age or even older and maybe not at all, because the money needed would increase in line with our ability to pay.

What we need is a way to think about time as an asset which can be valued in the same way as any other asset.

Try this as a thought experiment. Think of the years stretching ahead of you; write them down up to the year that you think represents a reasonable life expectancy. Now allocate a value to the current year, representing all the things you would do in a year. This is the value you put on your time. If you find it difficult to put a value on it, call it x if you wish. Now think about year 2. If you are told you would lose year 2 completely, how disappointed would you be now? What value would you put on year 2? And so on. You may find that as the years get later, you are putting a lower and lower value on them, because they are more remote, you will probably be able to do less, you may not even be around to enjoy them. So maybe it does make sense to use time now to achieve what we want, even if we have to work a bit longer at some time in the future.

Of course if we were asked in the future, the current year is likely to have the same value as any present year – it is just that because it is in the future it has less value for us now, just as the value of a pound now is worth more than a pound in ten years' time because we can invest it. So investing in ourselves by 5 years doing what we really want, would probably generate better health, closer friends, better relations with our partner if we have one, and have skills that we would not have acquired otherwise.

Now look at the value of any 5 years after age 65, and compare this value with any one year in the near future. If we are over 65, just take any 5 years in the future. We may well find that the value of 1 year now, is worth 5 years later on – in other words it may be a rational response to spend one year now doing what we really want, and this may give us more pleasure and happiness than 5 years of leisure sometime in the future. Indeed, it might even be worth doing some work for those 5 years if we have to in order to enjoy the time now. But it might just mean leaving a few thousand less to the taxman.

It might look like this :

Age	40	42	44	46	48	50	52	54	56	58
Value	100	80	70	61	52	44	37	31	26	22

Age	60	62	64	66	68	70	72	74	76	78
Value	19	17	16	15	15	15	15	15	15	15

This is an example of inconsistent 'hyperbolic discounting', where time closer to us is very much more valuable than even time a few years in the future – this is likely to lead to short term decisions. But everyone is different. If we were to discount time at a steady 5%/year it would look like this:

Age/Value

Age	40	42	44	46	48	50	52	54	56	58
Value	100	95	90	86	81	77	73	70	66	63

Age	60	62	64	66	68	70	72	74	76	78
Value	60	57	54	51	48	46	44	42	39	37

This puts a higher value on years ahead, and is likely to favour medium term decisions focusing on these years.

But what these examples indicate is that now the person finds one year of time now to be worth about 3- 6 years of time aged 78+. It may reflect a subjective feeling that by age 78, the things to do, the people to do them with and the overall satisfaction is significantly less than at age 40. There is no particular evidence this is correct – as we have seen age has only a very small effect on happiness, and what there is indicates that just after retirement, happiness can be high. What we are seeing is the discounted value of time then versus time now.

In other words, it may make sense to 'borrow' time from our long term retirement in order to invest it in what we want to do now. This investment may well pay off in terms of new skills, relationships, better health and may actually, just like a good investment 'pay for itself'.

Normal discounted cash flow needs to recognise that some things that have a payback well into the future are nonetheless essential. Examples might be sewage systems or even climate change initiatives which may only pay back in 100 years or longer. If these are subject to discounted cash flow, then they become uneconomic because the payback is so far in the future that when discounted, it becomes negligible. But they are still essential.

In the same way, we may decide on the basis of our values that certain activities or investments (in money, skills or life style) are so important to us that we will do them anyway, irrespective of when the payback is. Examples might include children, spiritual activities etc.

Mother and calf Whales that came to see us while we were swimming,
Tonga , Pacific 2005

26. The impact on others - Partner and Family

> We sailed 95% of our trip with friends; not only did this enable us to have a good night's sleep, and gave us back-up, it was also fun, and gave us the chance to share experiences. We were surprised by how few yachts crossing the Pacific had more than 2 people on them, some had just one. I think they are missing something...

Having got a clear statement of what we want to do, we have to (just like a business) work out how practical it is and the steps to achieving it. Included in this is working out the impact of this on those close to us – our family and friends.

I was lucky enough to have a partner who was excited by this dream of sailing away. And enough friends were keen enough to make it pretty clear that we would not have to lose touch with friends when we were away.

But plenty of other people who sail away have partners who are either sea sick or who hate the sea or who have other activity on land that they prefer. There is a good and a bad way to approach this and we have seen both. The bad way is to present it as an ultimatum – either you come with me, or we go our own way. The good way is to present it as a problem to be solved jointly – for example the land based partner flies out to meet the yacht at most ports, while the sailor arranges friends as crew. Or developing two mutually complementary roles in a new business for example. Or something similar.

The important point is that the goal is not seen as an unchangeable target. It only has meaning as long as it achieves what is desired and doesn't do more damage on the way than it's worth.

Try to think through what will be the reaction of people around us to what we are proposing before we do the proposing. This demonstrates that we do care about what they want and what effect our goals and actions have on them. Of course, they will probably have some angle that we haven't thought of, but provided we are not defensive about it, the chances of working it out and extracting the positive aspects of what they are saying, whilst minimizing the negative aspects, are quite good.

Of course we may find that it makes sense to help clarify what the other important people to us want themselves – their underlying motivators. This may then give us a real sense of being a team, and of being able to problem solve – to work out the best way of meeting everyone's motivations. Alternatively, at the very least we can ask others for their ideas and suggestions so that they are considered, rather than feeling ignored. That is not to say that we must always do whatever others want. But we give ourselves the best chance if we show that we value their input and consider it. This may sound like 'apple pie' – obvious and trite – but under stress it's the approach that is most likely to be forgotten with consequences that can wreck the otherwise best laid plans.

We have already reviewed the effect of marriage and cohabitation on happiness. What is less clear is the effect of one partner's work or not working on the other partner's happiness. Granted that marriage and cohabitation seems to increase the happiness of both partners, the interaction of work on happiness and life in general, means that a change of job or downsized work, or no job at all is likely to be a significant factor in both lives, which may increase or decrease the general level of satisfaction.

Just being at home together can cause problems particularly if one tries to critique or re-engineer the routines and habits of the other, or continually interrupting them. More than at any other time we need to allow personal space

There are many couples where only one person wants to undertake something as physically challenging as sailing; the other partner may well have other challenges for example their own work, full or part time, gardening, raising or care of children or grandchildren etc. It is the combination of these 2 'dreams' and 2 'realities' that is likely to determine whether the end result is seen to be beneficial. In other words, communication and clear goals are essential.

It will almost certainly involve negotiation to arrive at the best solution, with both partners being aware that the BATNA may well be separation. Which may motivate both to achieve a successful negotiation.

After all the change in circumstances from working in a high powered stressed job to a downsized one, to not working is likely to be extreme, and the old patterns of behaviour or even the old sharing of tasks or even the old division of power may no longer be appropriate.

Of course there is also the loss of friends from our current work to consider, unless we make significant efforts to retain communication with them. Social networking like Facebook and just email and websites can help to keep in touch, although not everyone will be interested in the new life style you are adopting – if nothing else it may represent a challenge to what they are doing, and their tactic may be to get even more immersed in work.

27. Change your job!

We had to enter Tiareroa Pass into Ahe Atoll in the Pacific during minimum outflow, and this is determined by the time of moonrise (there are no tide tables). The outflow begins at moonrise less 3 hours, reaches maximum outflow at the time the moon rises, then slackens before the inflow at Moonrise plus 5 hours. We had watched the (tiny) moon rise at 5am, so planned to be at the entrance at 8.30am. The atolls are so low and the charts so incomplete, that it is not even easy to make out which is the pass, but we threaded our way through the outlying reefs and were in the pass at 9.00am doing 1.5 knots against a 4.5 knot outflow. The depth shallowed to 2 metres, then we were through, and turned right towards the village 5 miles away. But Ahe atoll which used to trade copra (dried coconut) has now changed to make their living from cultivating black pearls which they sell to Japan. The farms are everywhere, with the oysters (tiny to large) strung on nylon ropes below the surface. We had to have Chris in the bow to spot these and the coral heads which could rip the keel from Intrepid if we hit one going too fast. With the sun behind us you can spot them, but they are not charted so it's all visual navigation.

There is a wide gap between theory and practice in changing jobs or stopping work. In theory any worker can at any time apply for any job. In practice, the range of options is much less – but nonetheless may still be much more than a 'boxed in' employee (or even someone unemployed) may consider. And if the need for income is reduced, and greater choices of location and hours allowed, then the opportunities will increase, although not all will maintain and improve our motivation.

So we may see a continuum running from full time high demand work through less stressed but more satisfying work to full time leisure. Personal control means deciding where we want to be on that continuum, and arranging things so that we stay motivated. Obviously much will depend on the particular job, our current skills and qualifications etc. There will be some trade-offs that will ultimately determine the sensible choice – although the emotional choice may be different.

Jobs can be characterized as being in

1. A location' eg London, Glasgow, New York
2. A Type of Business eg Oil Industry, Financial Services, Government
3. A Role eg Engineer, Analyst, Lawyer.

A 4th dimension would be overall remuneration and other benefits, a 5th would be hours of work required including commuting. These are the observable, objective measures of a job, in addition to the 10 factors already mentioned by Warr. They are also the ones likely to be mentioned early on by many workers eg when asked 'What do you do?' ('I am an engineer in the oil industry based in London'). In response to further questions they may tell us that the hours of work are Monday to Friday but require some weekend work, and later may tell us the salary (£60,000 say).

This engineer might draw up the following table to review options as to present job, different jobs or stopping work altogether, rating the 10 factors already identified on the basis to which they are met by each:

Factors	Present Job	Similar Job, Different Organisation	Different Job Same Business	Different Job, New Business	Retire ie Stop work
Location	London	Dubai	London	Working from home	Home or ...?
Business	Oil Industry	Oil Industry	Consultant to other organisations	Recruitment (probably for Oil Industry)	Personal Finance and Activities
Role	Engineer	Engineer	Consultant	Recruiter/ Head hunter	Arranging personal leisure and family life
Hours	50 + commuting	50 little commuting	60 + lots of travel	35 (60 + lots of travel but only for 8 months/year, so average 35)	None or lots
Pay etc	60,000	80,000	70,000	50,000	30,000 (Pension or investments)

Personal Control	Medium	Medium-low	High within assignments, but assignments are driven by clients.	High within assignments, but assignments are driven by clients.	High (provided income is high enough)
Opportunity for skills	High	Medium	High – but views may be ignored	High, but old skills not needed, new ones are.	High if well thought through
External goals	Demanding deadlines	Demanding deadlines	High – need to keep billable hours high and deliver results	High – need to meet demanding client requirements	Low, but internally generated goals high.
Variety	Varied tasks	Little variety	Varied	Varied, but essentially the same pattern each time. 4 months leisure can be very varied.	At our discretion
Clarity	Clear engineering standards, some ambiguity on cost/sustainable development	General engineering standards fairly clear, but ambiguous on costs, specific standards	Written brief, but often underlying ambiguity	Written brief but often underlying ambiguity and hidden agendas	Depends how well we have thought through our role.
Money	Budgets have to be proposed and are sometimes cut.	Money available but less influence on budgets	No real authority for money	Depends on client. Leisure activities may be costly or not.	Depends on wealth and income.
Physical Security	Usually good	Usually good	Fairly good but may be sent to dangerous locations	Good. Leisure activities may be dangerous but own choice	Probably high but ill health or dangerous environment possible …

Supportive Supervision	Conflict with Supervisor, but others good support	Not very supportive (less common ground)	General support but limited	Limited support. Leisure support depends on family	Depends on family
Interpersonal contact	Good but less than there used to be.	Adequate.	May be very lonely	Lots of contacts, but quality of interaction may be remote. Leisure depends.	Depends on how life style is set up
Valued social position	High perceived value (producing a needed commodity)	Medium (since operating out of own country)	Medium to low	Medium	Depends on role in retirement and what our peers are doing

What matters is:

1. being aware of and working through the options, 2. being aware of our own values and motivation and 'signature skills' – those that we truly feel define who we are, and that enable us to get into 'flow'; and 3. thinking through the consequences in a realistic way, avoiding the emotional features that may not actually have any real impact on our level of satisfaction.

These may include income, which as we have seen has not such a high impact provided it is 'adequate'; freedom to do what we want (which is not very valuable if we don't know what we want to do), pleasant environment (which is not very valuable if we don't actually appreciate it like the people who thought that moving to California would make them happier because of the better climate). On the other hand, if we value status then this is important and we will have to think carefully about what status we will have after the change – or at least see whether we can develop a new view on the world which pays less attention to status as defined by others, and more about status as defined by ourselves.

So we have the opportunity to explore many more options of what to do, without someone else structuring our life for us. Getting away from this structuring by others (or being tied by salary to an organisation) can be an intensely liberating experience – but it can also be a very scary one. All the things we have said that we might like to do – we can – there's no excuse, no reason not to do them. And the sheer choice can be bewildering – whereas moving to a new job usually requires having the right skills and qualifications, deciding to do something in leisure or after work does not usually come with the same stringent requirements – or at least with a bit of time (which we will have) and energy (which is up to us) we can train to meet them.

When it comes to stopping or downsizing work, here is a checklist of possibilities for generating some income without necessarily working full-time:

- Agent, Broker, Representative using your contacts to get clients, or putting together deals often on a no deal no fee basis
- Property. Buying properties cheap, possibly on auction, then redecorating or making major improvements, then selling or renting.
- Artist or sculptor. Not only does this engage talents you may not have had time to use properly before, it may well generate a good income.
- Volunteering or entering into a low pay high interest calling like Park Ranger, Hostel Warden, Church Vicar or similar, Assistant Golf Pro, Helper at Chandlery or Marina, Bar Tender, helping in the local shop, Brewmaster, Gardener.
- Direct investment in a small business – high tech cash devouring (which may mean that your investment gets so diluted that we don't get the fortune you hoped); or cash generating like a small retail store or garden centre or other retail service which may be a better bet.
- Working for your previous organisation as a part time advisor, recruiter, cv screener, peak workload cover.
- Sabbatical or reduced hours for anything from 3 months to 2 years or even more. If there is a downturn in demand the organisation will be keener to offer one, but even in high demand, if we are

going to resign anyway, they may prefer to offer a sabbatical to keep contact.

- Writing – this can be anything from articles for the local paper, to novels or non fiction. It can be difficult to get a publisher, use personal contact rather than mass mailings.
- Teaching. There is often a high demand for Maths, Science and Technology teachers for example, and engineers or technologists can give something back. There are often grants to help with training that may be needed.
- Consultant or freelance using our skills and contacts to help other organisations including our previous employer and clients or Private Equity. Either independent or associated with others, may well involve due diligence and valuing possible deals.
- Bed and breakfast or holiday rents. This reduces our flexibility and will need care about insurance and regulations, but can provide useful income.
- Start our own small business – selling a coin collection, selling garden plants, selling on eBay for others, stripping antiques, organic produce, restaurant, vineyard etc. This could be started while working full time, perhaps with our partner doing some of the work, while we work during evenings, only stopping full time work when the business has grown.
- Non-executive director using our contacts to help the businesses to gain contracts, finance and have the best strategic direction, and/ or audit or remuneration committee. These maintain some status trappings, so are particularly good if this is a concern. FT.com has a website specifically for this.
- Magistrate or local council.
- Taking a University course, perhaps a Masters; and we may even be asked to lecture or tutor on subsequent courses.

Of course, for every door that we open, most of the other doors close – at least for the time being. If we decide to sail around the world, we cannot usually also do a full time job or climb Mount Everest or create a natural garden. And the longer we stay away from full time organizational based work the more difficult it will be to re-enter, both because of our own motivation, and the need to persuade any new organization that even if our skills are up to date, our hearts are also committed to the work. But I was able to return to work full time for a major FTSE 100 organisation after 7 years away sailing, so it is possible.

So a decision to stop work or downsize is not to be taken lightly – it is not irreversible, but it has the makings to be.

There are ways to limit this irreversibility – sabbaticals, temporary reduced hours, temporary assignments, consulting, freelancing, contracting, non-executive directorships, etc, are all ways to stay in contact and make the change less of a gulf. If we have a partner (romantic or otherwise) it may be possible for them to start a business while we only contribute when we can eg in vacations or weekends. This is a very good way to test the water. The time saved in commuting to work can often make this very efficient, we may get 11 hours of work done from home on something we want instead of 8 hours work at the office.

But some of these methods also can limit our freedom. It is possible to freelance while sailing the Pacific, but do we really want to be hammering away at a report or code down below when the whole reason for wanting to go sailing the Pacific is around us on deck? And are we going to be as competent and switched on to latest developments when our communications may be coming in on a deadly slow link which usually fails halfway through? The stress inherent in this may be as bad as working full time – without the same financial rewards. And we will not have the 'risk it all' mentality that guarantees 100% effort to make it work.

We will not be alone in this, and there are plenty of examples to learn from. In UK and USA about 25% of people aged 30-59 have voluntarily made changes that resulted in them earning less money. In the UK the reduction in income was 40% on average. So it makes a lot of sense to ask others for their experiences before we embark on our own journey. The best people to ask will be people you know – think widely, and be prepared to ask – most people love being asked about their experiences and feedback.

What we need is to test the boundaries and how practical our ideas are. This is covered in the next chapter.

Bernard enjoying work life balance

28. Testing the Boundaries – downsizing and sabbaticals

> The longest holiday Denis had ever taken before now was 1 week. So taking 5 weeks was something special for him, and for Elaine.

Some people work until the day they die – and this makes perfect sense if they love their work. However, suppose you don't love your work – it is perhaps OK, some good times, some bad times, the rest all right; frustrations with the travel to and from work, inconsistent bosses, soulless offices or factories, and missing family or leisure events that we would like to attend. Possibly relations with our boss are not brilliant, and our organisation seems to be continually ratcheting up what we are required to do, so that every time we meet a target, the next one is even tougher, and the resources we have reduced. Strategy changes frequently so we do not feel at all in control of what we are doing. We often feel stressed because of this, yet the income is pleasant.

Recognise this? Should we aim to work until the day we die? Well, from a purely selfish point of view, the answer is probably no, if we are being rational about it (after all no-one on their death bed ever said they wished they had spent more time at work). This is because there are probably other activities that we prefer doing to work (on average) and at some point (which may be early or quite late in life), we will probably have acquired enough wealth or income to be able to do these activities without needing the income from work. (We may get a reduced income from a pension or equivalent or part time work instead). Additionally, we know that our health is unlikely to stay the same, and many activities that may be on our wish list are dependent on a reasonable degree of fitness – or at least are more enjoyable if we are healthy and fit.

So when are we going to change or stop? People usually over-estimate how much they can achieve in one year; and under-estimate how much they can achieve in a decade, so using a time frame of at least 5-10 years is much better strategically than one year, although it is wise to only commit to being away from work for one year at first if this is possible.

Well the first thought exercise we might try is to imagine whether there is any work that indeed would genuinely be so absorbing and satisfying that we would like to do it until the day we die. Bill Deedes the journalist was reporting from locations as difficult as Darfur in Sudan the week before he died aged 94. What is interesting is that he had been a cabinet minister and editor of a national paper, yet he was willing to 'downsize' to a role (reporter) that he could continue in and enjoyed doing more than anything else (because if he didn't enjoy doing it he would presumably have done something else or nothing).

It's a useful thought exercise to consider all the many roles we might have or work we might do which we would REALLY enjoy doing – especially because it is likely that the financial demands reduce as any children we have become independent, mortgages are paid off, and alternative sources of income from pensions or savings become available.

One of the more interesting considerations is that the classic 40 hours/ week, 48 weeks/year job often presents us with a stark choice between all or nothing work, whereas what we would like in an ideal world is ... greater control over our working hours. So this may be one consideration. Is there work that will enable us to make a contribution, generate an income (perhaps smaller), and yet give us more freedom? Non-executive directorships, part time consultancy, advisors to small or large firms, self employment, trading shares, real estate development or refurbishment, satisfying independent projects that make a little money or at least save costs are all possible.

Of course there are other considerations including how able are we to do the work? We all know people who carried on beyond the time when they were the best person for the job. Sir Winston Churchill was a great man, but many people think that he carried on in the twilight of his career when he would have done better to hand over to someone else, indeed when the country was harmed by him staying in power.

And Mao Tse Tung made some appalling decisions at a time late in his life when he was a long way from being the best person to lead China. Thus Bill Deede's last role was a particularly good one, in that if people don't agree with what you have reported, they are free to ignore it, whereas there are many roles which have a major capacity to harm the prospects, motivation and wealth of others if occupied by someone who is only there out of habit or the triumph of the status quo. First do no harm.

What does the happiness evidence have to say about downsizing? Well, it may well be better than just stopping, especially if the stopping is involuntary. Becoming unemployed reduces happiness by some 6%. However, if becoming unemployed is voluntary, then the effect is much less and may even be positive as we gain personal control over our life. Downsizing may give us the best of worlds, some income, better tax rates, and satisfaction if we choose well. It will also force us to keep our brains active which is important for long term health if nothing else.

There is no point in stopping work if we just work harder than ever at saving money – if our whole world revolves around saving a few dollars or pounds or getting the very best value for everything. This is not living, this is misery. So we need to be clear on our real goal, and what money we need to sensibly progress towards this. It may be helpful to think what one hour is worth to us in this new situation. Suppose that we could earn £20 for one hours work; or just as likely save £30 by doing something ourselves rather than paying someone to do it, or by queuing or working the web for one hour to get a bargain £30 cheaper. Is this worth it? Suppose we saved £100 for one hour? Or £10? We will probably work out a rule of thumb as to how much our time is worth if we have to do things that do not contribute to what we really want to do but nonetheless save money.

Of course, we still have the element of personal control. Part time work may carry requirements which mean that we still cannot be away for more than a week or so at a time; and it may involve the same investment in skills knowledge and networking as a full time job – but with the payback much less because the work is part time. On the other hand, we may be able to arrange affairs so that the downsized work is largely under our personal control, in which case the chances of our downsizing leading to increased happiness are much greater.

When we are considering a change of job, we may well find that in the real world there do not seem to be any jobs that would give us what we want – certainly none that we would be likely to be accepted into. This presents us with a challenge – we may be clear about what we want, but if we can't get it, then all we have done is increase our sense of frustration. Of course, some people would say that if we are REALLY committed to our goal and persevere at it long enough eventually we will achieve it. But in practice this is simply not true. Consider, just to take one example, athletes and footballers, some of whom win gold medals or achieve high paying jobs, but for every one who makes it there are hundreds who do not – for whatever reason, be it injury or simply other people having better skills.

This is not meant to be encouragement to give up, far from it, just that the most fulfilled people may well be those who work out how to move on from setbacks, rather than kicking a closed door. The way to move on from setbacks, may well be to recognise the skills and competencies we have, (including new ones acquired in pursuit of the original goal) then to relax one or more of the boundary conditions or aspects of the goal, so that we create a new goal for ourselves that will stretch us and use our skills.

One key boundary condition that can be relaxed or changed when someone is close to being able to stop work, or downsize, is the need for a large income from employment. If this requirement is relaxed, then many other opportunities that will be both motivating and satisfying and useful may become possible. In other words, if we do not have to earn a large salary we may be able to develop new ideas, retrain to gain new skills, start new projects etc.

But if we do this, are we being lazy or not contributing to society? This is explored in the next chapter.

Intrepid from the Masthead in the Maldives

29. Are Happychondriacs a threat to society?

> 'One of the great rewards of moving from the disassembling period (midlife) to renewal is coming to approve of oneself morally and ethically and quite independent of others' standards and agenda' ('Passages' by Gail Sheehy).

If more people genuinely pursued their own happiness rather than a larger income, what are the implications? Well, if people leave highly paid jobs to undertake something else that they think they would enjoy more and which better fitted their goal in life, (perhaps on a lower income, perhaps on no earned income at all), there would presumably be less produced, and less consumed (assuming that the work done is productive (in some cases this is not necessarily true). There would be less tax paid (because income would be lower), and fewer jobs created because there would be less demand (less money being spent).

There is also likely to be less stress related illness, and hence less money required for health services, (which in private health systems would lower private sector demand, in UK's National Health Service this would mean a reduction in government spending). Younger people would be promoted, so there may be increased productivity (depending on the judgment of the people concerned), and increased motivation (many firms rely on growth to provide for promotions required to motivate their younger stars).

However, there may also be a contrast effect to reduce motivation – if those remaining have to work long hours while those who have left are sunning themselves abroad. This may be motivating ('I can leave early as well if I only work hard now') or de-motivating ('It's just not fair!').

If the people leaving full-time work go abroad, then the country they are leaving will suffer a further reduction in demand (the lower income won't even be spent here, but will be in most cases be spent abroad). On the other hand, other countries will benefit, so there may be some element of, if not overseas aid, then at least overseas development.

The main effect may well be an increase in individual output. Some people may join not for profit organisations, or government in a variety of roles. But the main emphasis may well be on individual action and roles, to achieve the sense of freedom that is often the driving force that lead us to 'do our own thing' in the first place.

Is it selfish to do our own thing? Well, in a way it depends as it has for most of our life on who 'we' are? Is 'we' really 'I' only? Or is it ourselves as a couple? Or is 'we' including any children we have, and our parents? Or does 'we' include close friends, or our local community or our country or people in general?

When we were at school, we were mostly studying and developing (and playing etc) for our own benefit as we could see (dimly at first) that we needed to get through certain milestones in order to be a fully functioning adult. Later, in our twenties, we would regard ourselves mostly as an individual but involved with others, contributing as we could, so that we were pretty selfish, but usually aware that we could not totally ignore others (at work and leisure) in our decisions. Later 'We' may become a 'couple' (temporary or longer), and later there may be children, so there are family and wider financial demands in addition to work demands, community demands etc.

In part it may be these demands that we feel constrains our freedom. To misquote Ralph Waldo Emmerson: 'We are not being self-reliant, because we are too cluttered with a wide variety of demands, and certainly don't feel in control of our own lives'.

At this point we may reconsider. Do we want to continue in this work, or move to something else or stop working for others altogether? Some people may conclude that 'we' means 'I' – just that – and decide what is best for me. But it is never that simple, if nothing else does it mean 'I' in the short term (I want to go stop work and go away and lie on a beach or whatever?) but this has implications for medium and long term (It may mean that I am bored lonely and poor later on, in which case I have not even optimized my strategy for myself).

Or we may conclude that we can relax or release the demands of work and children (they may have left home and become self-sufficient so that our interaction with them relaxes) but 'we' still includes our partner (if we have one), close friends, our children (but less strong than before), our parents (if still around), perhaps our local community, perhaps some parts of our profession if not the specific to the last company we worked for.

This is still more than enough relaxation of demands to enable a wide ranging review of the options open to 'us', so that without retreating into navel gazing introspection or undiluted hedonism, we may nonetheless arrive at a new plan for what 'we' want to do, that gives us most of what we want, including the interaction and support for partner, friends, children, community etc. And of course, we may be on the receiving end of this, (hopefully involved but we may have to fight our corner for that), so that our partner or someone else close to us decides to make a career change which has big implications for us and others close to them.

Put this way, whilst it's probably selfish and almost certainly short sighted to focus exclusively on what 'I' want to do, provided we are sensible enough to take a broader focus on 'we' and to recognise that our own needs and wants probably include others (as they have in the past), then it is no more selfish to review what 'we' want to do in the light of changing demands on us, than at any other time in the past.

Indeed, as we get older and less fit, there may be some ways in which our best contribution to wider society is to make ourselves as far as we can 'self-reliant' so that we are not making demands on others. So there is a real sense of a social contract here – as demands on me weaken (in terms of work and financial support of children for example), I will in turn work to make myself as robust as I can, so that I do not make more demands on society or my children or my partner than is positive and healthy – in other words, by no means to cut off contact, (if anything to increase it), but rather to do my best to contribute rather than demand from others. Ideally this is what we really want to do anyway, but if not then at least we can negotiate a path that optimizes what we do in terms of our definition of who 'we' are living for.

It's interesting that Ralph Waldo Emerson paid such attention to fulfilling ourselves and becoming more or less 'independent' rather than trying to help others. Have you ever wondered at some helpers or charities who sometimes seem to do more harm than good, well intentioned people or organisations that all too often create muddle and muddy the waters or who create incentives for the people they are trying to help that are actually counter-productive?

A very simplified example might be giving money to someone who is out of work. Laudable, but if too much money is given, then the incentive to work is taken away, as is the incentive to learn skills to enable work anyway. Another might be giving to charitable or not for profit organisations whose executives seem to spend more time and energy arranging their own futures and positions, and basing themselves in attractive and high cost locations like Geneva, rather than benefitting the stated beneficiaries. Or giving aid to governments whose corrupt ministers channel the money to their own pockets or to arms; or where an increasing number of charities are competing amongst themselves for money and handouts, so the net effect of all that effort actually does very little to increase the total benefit achieved.

This is not to say that helping others is wrong, just that if the vehicle used is so inefficient that it creates more confusion than help, then we are better off looking after ourselves, and in Emerson's terms, working to become self-reliant ourselves, so we can help others when there are genuine opportunities to do so, and when it fits our own sense of what we are on earth to do.

And it is precisely that sense of what we are here for that needs to be clarified, if we are not to fall into the trap of Happychondria – a self-centred focus on making myself happy. The other negative to be avoided is a self-centred focus on getting more status and consumer goods in the deluded belief that this will make us happy or (even more deluded) help others.

So we need to be clear on what we enjoy and what we are trying to do. But then having clarified this, to record it, and use it to guide our life, not to have the process endlessly re-worked so that we end up so self-centred that we become Happychondriac, often introverted, and fail to find the very happiness we are so assiduously searching for.

A strategic review is good so long as it creates a clear and hopefully better strategy, but a strategic review that never ends creates only muddle and mess. People need to have a sense of control, that if some action works well today it will probably be the right thing to do tomorrow.

Recall that too many choices seems to create unhappiness rather than contentment, and evaluating each action in terms of what will make us happy is likely to make us more confused than ever because there are an almost limitless choice of actions, and trying to decide which will make us happy (even if we could do it for just a few of the options) is not really practical or even the way we behave.

Even if we are not an extravert, there may be a way to increase our happiness without focusing on it. We may either take a strategic look and regard happiness as the overall goal, but not the specific objective, so we may for example examine what factors contribute most to our happiness (like tactical objectives) then get on with pursuing these objectives. To use a military analogy, we may aim to win the battle, or take the hill, and not worry too much about the overall war. Or we may identify an overall purpose to our life, and pursue this, and happiness may come along as a by-product. The success of this latter strategy is likely to depend on the choice of purpose. It is even possible that any single purpose is too simplistic, and that to live a happy fulfilled life we need a number of goals. Maybe the driven blinkered person is the only real loser in life, however successful in the single goal they have set themselves. The exercises in Chapter 25 are designed to arrive at a number of goals or wants, rather than a single abstract overarching mission.

So we normally end up living in a sense of habit, doing what comes naturally to us because we did it yesterday, or because we have a daily or weekly or monthly or yearly routine, and we may review this occasionally, but let's not spend every day asking ourselves what will make us happiest. Life is too short. And if we do focus too much on short term happiness, we may well end up using or abusing drugs ranging from Alcohol to Cannabis to Ecstasy to Heroin to Modafinil or Ritalin (the last 2 prescription drugs sometimes abused for other purposes to enhance our cognitive ability). This opens up a whole area of ethical issues on human enhancement which respected advisory bodies including the RSA are grappling with.

For now, though we need some more practical rules or habits to guide us, to make us happy or get us into 'flow' or make us usually content or whatever we decided we want to achieve.

And these may well be the activities and attributes we identified in the tables in Chapters 21 and 22 and in Chapter 25 – physical activities like sports or gardening or leisure or dance, talking with friends, being in and contributing to a community we trust, interacting with a partner (if we are lucky enough), doing activities which we know give us the best chance to be fulfilled and to get 'in the flow', and generally seizing the positive opportunities that come up, and not worrying too much about the negative events because we don't feel the need or cause to blame ourselves (or others) for them, and anyway they probably won't happen again (especially if we arrange things to avoid this).

So we can be true to ourselves, doing what we really want to do, increasing our own self-reliance as our contribution to the community as a whole, and helping others when we are best fitted to do so and in ways that play to our strengths. This means not being an ever increasing consumer because of habit alone and because we can't think of anything better to do. Because there are better things to do...

Wahaiba Sands at sunset, Oman

30. Conclusion

The psychology of happiness and well-being is complex because all the factors overlap so it's difficult to see the effect of any factor in isolation; causation is often two way and is usually confused; our memory and anticipation are fallible; and self-reports on happiness are swayed by short term events. In addition, most of the effects are reported as the average effect – not much use to those of us who are not average. There are also real limits to what we can change even if we wanted to. That is the bad news.

On the other hand, we are at least better informed knowing this, and if we take it into account we will make better decisions. We are encouraged to have the confidence to work out what we really want to do, to appreciate that beyond a certain point higher income is unlikely to have much effect on how happy we are. We need to realise that the material values and products we are continually exhorted to have by status seekers and marketing are unlikely even to provide us with a higher income, let alone make us happier. Conversely close relationships with co-workers, friends, children, partner, spouse, neighbours (the more groupings the better) are all likely to make us happy and healthier, (and this benefits both parties), and helping others may well be a key part of what we want to do. Formal ties like marriage help to increase happiness by reinforcing our personal control, but separation can adversely affect our happiness and also that of our children long term. Active sports, dance, other activities, pets etc are beneficial to happiness as well as to health, so although we cannot easily change our personality, we can to some extent change the way we explain success and failure, how we think about things, and our values and our behaviour.

Our work may well be as satisfying as our leisure, in which case stick with it and enjoy the journey. But if our work is not satisfying (over a reasonable period – everyone has bad days and even bad months or years), then it makes sense to see what we can do about it, and not let cognitive dissonance or the distorting effect of remuneration lead us to over-value work that may genuinely be bad for us. We may find that we do not have a sense of being in control of our lives or our work and it is this very powerful factor that is causing us to be unhappy. If so, then we may consider alternatives including those which involve a lower income for fewer hours or more satisfaction provided it is still above about $24,000 (about £18,000) /head. Because we have learned that we adapt rapidly to new circumstances, and the effect of changes in income on happiness is only about 3%, any loss of income is very likely to be overwhelmed by a greater sense of personal control if we are really doing what we want.

Many people put off thinking about what they want because they fear it will cost too much and instead focus in a blinkered way on acquiring money until ill health or circumstances forces them to change, in which case the involuntary nature of the change and the time lost may well mean that many opportunities have closed and the sense of being out of control during the change is likely to make us unhappy or depressed.

If we strip away much of the 'froth' from our spending, and aim to become more self-reliant, the income we need may be much less than we originally thought; the capital to provide this may be estimated by using the 4 or 5% rule, and because tax and other costs reduce significantly, we may already have this. This wealth can also act as a 'vaccine' against depression, reminding us that we retain our personal control, and reducing the effect of adverse events that could be traumatic if we did not have a cushion. Like any change, careful thought is needed especially gaining information from others who have done something similar, (because although we are unique, we also have lots of similarities), and if there are opportunities to trial the change eg by sabbaticals, part time work, moonlighting, vacations etc these should be seized.

Our thought processes and happiness are swayed by fallible memory, momentary moods, adaptation and material values. Our Personality, Relationships, Purpose and Self Reliance are more important for long term happiness and contentment than high income or status possessions, and we probably need less income to be happy than we think. We can change the way we think about life, and how we live it, and knowledge of the psychology of happiness will enable us to make better decisions about how we live our life than just habit.

Aleppo Soukh 2008; now rubble, a human tragedy

31. FOOTNOTE – INTREPID

Intrepid of Dover was built in 2000, while I was still working for Ernst and Young International. The yard constructing her went bankrupt when she was about 80% complete, which gave us our first taste of the challenges to come. The choice of name comes from this time, and it is instructive that our first challenges were legal and financial rather than as we had anticipated, bad weather and storms. Fortunately, we had insisted on a contract which gave us legal possession of what we had paid for, and we were able to have her finished in another yard to a good standard. Nicky and I tested Intrepid with friends over the next year, then sailed her down to the Canaries during the summer and autumn of 2001.

The events of 9/11 just reinforced my decision to sail, and Ernst and Young were good enough to offer me a one-year sabbatical. We held a party to brief our friends on what we were proposing to do, and within 24 hours had almost all the friends as crew we needed.

We joined the ARC (Atlantic Rally for Cruisers) which gave us confidence as up to that point, I had only sailed 4 weeks on the ocean in my life (in chartered boats). We crossed the Atlantic (2700 miles) in 20 days, cruised up to Florida, then back across the Atlantic where I had to decide whether to continue sailing or not. Really it was no contest – I advised EY that I was resigning, we turned south and spent one year in the Med, (to be closer to our son James who was in his first year of University), then re-crossed the Atlantic in 2003, headed up through Puerto Rico and the east coast of the USA to New York, (sailing past the remains of the twin towers), then down through Key West and onto Panama and the Pacific where many of the excerpts from our log begin. We crossed the Pacific in 2005, and after Australia sailed north through Indonesia to Thailand, Sri Lanka, the Maldives and up the Red Sea where the introduction to this book was written. Intrepid was then based in Turkey, and we explored Syria and Lebanon. I joined Man Group (a major hedge fund), in 2008 and worked full time for a period, then in 2010 sailed down the west coast of Africa to Gambia, and crossed the Atlantic again to South America, just north of the moth of the Amazon, and up the coast to Trinidad. From there we explored the Caribbean, and then sailed north to New York and Cape Cod, before returning to the Caribbean in 2016.

We held to 6 principles when planning the trip:

1. We would enjoy ourselves, and seize the unrivalled opportunities we had. Where money was needed to enjoy wherever we were, or to stay in touch with family (tours, guides, flights etc) we spent it.

2. We would stay in touch with our family and friends – our son James came along for the first 2 Atlantic crossings and then came out to wherever we were during vacations. I flew back to see my mother every 6 months or so; we had a satellite phone so phoned every week; and we had friends with us for 42,000 of the 45,000 miles we have sailed so far. We emailed our friends every 2 weeks or so, and this inspired a number to join us or do something similar.

3. We would stay within budget. We rented out our main residence to supplement our income, and with this and other bits were able to actually finish our trip with roughly the same money as we started with, because accommodation on Intrepid is 'free' apart from maintenance and depreciation. We shared food costs with friends who were with us at the time, but made no other charges.

4. We would try to be as self-reliant as we could. Partly this was forced on us, because good professionals are rare anywhere, and we had to be able to mend things in mid ocean.

5. We would manage our risks. We did this by starting with a sabbatical, buying a tested seaworthy boat, joining the ARC (which included safety and equipment checks), following a route which kept us away from hurricane zones at the time of year we were there, and by having a full medical kit and friends with us, so that when for example Nicky broke her arm in mid-Atlantic, the other 4 of us managed fine, and between us set the bone so well it needed little further treatment. We also insured Intrepid and had travel insurance.

6. We would retain our roots – we did not sell our house, we kept in touch with friends and family by blogging, and have returned to our home village and pub and friends

Many people who live their dream, don't involve their partner or children (for a variety of reasons). The most common one is that the partner or children don't like the activity, or has other commitments. This is not necessarily a deal-breaker, because it is possible to limit the involvement eg sail with friends as crew and for the partner to fly out to meet them at suitable places. It just needs negotiation.

Generally, we found that people sailing by themselves weren't keen to have other people on board, and 90% of the yachts crossing the Pacific had just 2 people on board which seems a shame. Although we met people along the way, the opportunity to have some long term friends actually sailing with us seemed too good to miss, and we worked hard to arrange this. Of course it introduces an element of schedule, because friends are often working and have to arrange time off, but the benefit of enjoying friends while sailing is significant.

The depreciation and cost of maintenance for Intrepid is about £8,000 – £15,000 pounds per year, but against this we have 'free' or very cheap accommodation anchored or moored in the centre of some of the finest cities in the world (NY, Washington DC, Baltimore, Miami, Marseille, Nice, Rome, Naples, Tahiti, Brisbane, Darwin, Singapore, Aden) or of course, some remote Pacific island that you can only get to by boat...

The cover photograph was taken when we were going through the Suez Canal, and found ourselves pursuing a large tanker named ... Great Happy. Such a coincidence was too much, and pursuing happiness was the inevitable conclusion.

Man with mobile on camel, Syria
2008

Appendix 1. The distorting effect of market forces and some remuneration schemes

Final salary pension plans (defined benefit) have the effect of significantly leveraging the benefits if the person works until retirement, since the typical formula of (years worked x final salary /60) or similar has a major increase in value in the last few years because of the double multiplier of years and salary. Consider (in real terms):

Years worked in Organisation	Salary	Pension at Pension Age	Value of Pension over 25 years
5	£20,000	£1,600	£40,000
10	£30,000	£5,000	£125,000
20	£40,000	£13,300	£332,500
30	£50,000	£25,000	£625,000

For this person living 25 years beyond pension age, the effect of working that last 10 years is £292,000 in extra pension or almost a doubling of yearly income.

What effect does this have on moving jobs in mid-career? Suppose we work for Organisation A for 15 years, then join Organisation B for the next 15 years, both having similar schemes, so work the same 30 years.

Company	Years worked	Final Salary	Pension at Pension Age	Value of Pension over 25 years
A	15	£35,000	£8,750 (15x35/60)	£219,000
B	15	£50,000	£12,500(15x50/60)	£312,000
Total	30		£21,250	£531,000

So although we work the same years, on the same salary, the pension is 15% lower, £3,750 less/year, (£21,250 rather than £25,000/year, or £94,000 less over 25 years) compared to someone who stays with the same organisation for all 30 years.

Defined contribution schemes while significantly less generous to the employee do not provide the same distortion, and enable greater flexibility, but still encourage working longer because of the compounding effect on the capital value, and the enhanced pension the later it is taken.

Tax will have a major effect, and can produce similar incentives/disincentives when we consider what work we want to do, and what the effect will be on our income. Inflation and security of provider are also major considerations that will skew our 'rational' decision on what is best. It is beyond the scope of this book to go into the detailed financial analysis, but the status quo may be just as risky as change. Doing nothing is not always the best or even the safest approach.

Incentive schemes and share options can also have a major effect on decision making:

These examples show how organisations and their advisors may unintentionally skew the judgment of people who work for them.

In the UK and USA especially, the increasing dominance of the financial sector has brought with it a different model of compensation. Earlier manufacturing and indeed most industries before 1980's had compensation policies which broadly set pay at the lowest rate that could be negotiated or set, and bore little relationship to overall profitability of the organisation. The reason for this was that if pay was explicitly set in relation to profits, then whilst in bad years there was a strong justification for low increases, in good years there would be little justification not to share the profit with the workers. Since pay was largely basic salary, this could lead to uncompetitive pay levels during subsequent hard times.

The financial sector and especially investment banks used a different model, perhaps because there is less need for major shareholder investment in plant and machinery. In investment banks a large proportion of profits (50% say), was set aside for distribution to the workers (or partners) usually in the form of bonuses, so that if profits were low next year, so would be bonuses. This model has gradually extended to all organisations, and private equity is extending the idea even further by direct investment of key workers in the enterprise thereby side-lining shareholders altogether, and increasing the wealth and income of the top 5% of workers.

Shareholders have been persuaded to compete with this by offering ever higher bonuses to CEO's and other directors. This emphasis on variable pay can however produce strange consequences. One example has hit the headlines recently. Senior executives including the CEO are usually incentivised (awful word, but it's the one commonly used by the consultants who set these schemes up), by various share option plans and bonuses determined by financial targets. The targets and share options are usually best met by increasing revenue and profit growth. Now suppose there are 2 strategic options open to us, and the consequences are shown in the table, where the first figure is the result for the CEO, the 2nd for the Company:

CEO/Organisation

Strategy	Steady low risk growth 90% success likely	Dramatic high risk profit growth eg Acquisition or major cost cutting on maintenance, staff, investment etc 40% success likely *
Result if it succeeds	CEO: + $1m Org: +$100 m	CEO: +$20 million Org: +$500 million
Result if it Fails	CEO: $0.5m Org: $0 m	CEO: $0million Org: -$500 million

More acquisitions fail to increase shareholder value than increase it over the medium-long term, so 40% is not unrealistic.

What should the rational CEO to increase his/her income? Well multiplying the probability by the outcome, gives this expected return:

Strategy	Steady Growth	Acquisition
CEO	+$0.95m	+$ 8m
Company	+$90m	-$100m

So the rational CEO is on average $7,100,000 better off if he takes the risky option, even though the probability based outcome for the organisation is negative by $100 million. Part of the problem is that everyone will argue that 'their' strategy is not really risky at all and is sure (or highly likely) to succeed.

Even if the chance of success of the risky high growth strategy is known to be 10%, the incentives still encourage the CEO to gamble with other people's money. The expected pay-out to the CEO and company at 10% chance of success is still to encourage the CEO to take the risk because they gain £1,100,000, even though the probability is that the Company will lose $400m.

Strategy	Steady Growth	Acquisition/High risk growth 10% success
CEO	+$0.95 million	+$2 million
Company	+$90 million	-$400 million

The rational CEO will certainly be motivated to make the risky strategy succeed, once the decision has been taken. But at the point of decision, the incentives shown here have the effect of dramatically encouraging strategies which have a very low chance of success, because the rational selfish CEO, to maximize his/her expected income and wealth (which is what incentive schemes are there for) should choose the risky acquisition or dramatic cost cutting strategy, (gaining an average of $7.1 million in the first case) whereas the best option for the Company is the steady growth strategy (gaining $190 million over the alternative).

Of course, there are limits and conditions, including usually time limits before the options mature, or the incentive is collected, and the gain to the Company in for example, share price may be greater over the longer term, (so may the losses). However, the real problems often don't come to light for a bit, and if the company is the target of a bid, (as is the case half the time), then the increased share price usually pays off very quickly for the executives (and the non-executive remuneration committee directors). So advisors will specifically target the executives to encourage them to back the bid.

You think this is unreal? Let me just quote Alvin Offner a respected Professor at Oxford University and expert in Economic History: "The rise in executive pay in the US and UK has reached such multiples of average earnings that have alarmed even Business Week. Remuneration bears little relation to economic performance, and is influenced by the reciprocal gifting motives of compensation committee members"

This is interesting because other studies have indicated that where executives have a significant share ownership in the organisation they work for, they are much <u>less</u> likely to over-pay for a target acquisition than if they only own a small number of shares in their organisation. This is consistent with private equity or management buy-out approaches where the drive is often to get the executives to own a large number of shares and/or to take on large debt – not so much to finance the transaction, but rather to motivate them at the same time trying to ensure judgments are not skewed to personal gain over Company benefit.

One successful entrepreneur told me that his secret of success is to 'Risk Everything'. This way, since the consequences of failure are so awful (the end of everything he values) he will subject the decision to such careful scrutiny; and when committed will move heaven and earth to make it succeed. To date his formula has worked, perhaps because he has so much at personal risk. If did not have so much at personal stake he would not be so careful.

If we wanted to match the results for the CEO and the organisation, we should insist that the CEO buys about $40 million shares in the organisation and retains them for 5 – 10 years, so that if they halve in value after the acquisition, his or her wealth is reduced by about $20 million – about the same loss as the incentive if the acquisition worked; so that there is no artificial incentive to risk. If a CEO takes the job under these conditions, we could be very sure that they have weighed every risk. But it will be tough to persuade them to take the job.

Of course, it could be argued that business needs to take risks, and stagnation is no panacea either, and that anything that encourages risk taking is good. That's fine provided the risk is accompanied by the motivation and care consistent with the consequences for the organisation.

ACKNOWLEDGEMENTS

Martin Seligman was a Professor in Pennsylvania doing ground breaking work on learned helplessness while I was at Bryn Mawr, PA, studying evolutionary psychology on a Fulbright Scholarship. Professor Seligman is now a leading advocate of Positive Psychology, and was my first inspiration. Daniel Kahneman was the first psychologist to gain the Nobel prize for Economics, and I have huge admiration for the way he has combined the study of behaviour so as to draw out the lessons for business and professional practice. He also co-edited the seminal work on Happiness or Well Being (with Ed Diener, and Norbert Schwarz). Richard (Lord) Layard is a distinguished economist who has made the journey in the opposite direction, examining the psychology of Happiness with a particular emphasis on the implications for Government. We have to hope that his conclusions have the effect on Government policy that they should have. Daniel Nettle specializes in Personality at the University of Newcastle, and provided rare insight into this thorny subject. Ed Diener does the same from the other side of the Atlantic. The BBC has found itself under attack at different times, but its unique take on 'How to be Happy' (the book is edited by Liz Hoggard) was a brave and insightful attempt to take the subject into the community. Daniel Gilbert is Professor at Harvard and his recent book Stumbling on Happiness (which won the prize for best Science Book) reminds us of the fallibility of our thought processes, whilst entertaining us with double entendres throughout.

Two Britons were researching important aspects of this subject well before it was even called Happiness – Michael Argyle from the viewpoint of social psychology, and Peter Warr on job satisfaction, and both have made significant contributions.

The literature on NLP is extensive and represents another practical way to use many of the techniques, some developed in psychology, others from a variety of sources, which all have the common thread that they demonstrably work in the real world, outside the psychology lab. I will not list all the works here, but they are readily available.

Shell and Ernst and Young were good enough to pay me to do what I enjoyed doing, and to explore my practice of business psychology. Man Group were that rarity in financial services, an enlightened employer who strove to maintain a satisfying work life balance.

My thanks go to the friends who sailed with us in Intrepid of Dover and made what could have been an exhausting trial into an exhilarating and fun trip – all 50,000 miles of it. They are listed on <u>www.intrepidofdover.co.uk</u>, which covers the trip around the world, as are the complete ships logs and photos.

Lastly my wife Nicky and son James were brave enough to trust themselves to a psychologist who had to transform himself into a sailor and more importantly maintainer of boats in mid ocean, and thereby made it all possible.

CPSIA information can be obtained
at www.ICGtesting.com
Printed in the USA
LVOW06s0843041216
515734LV00028B/205/P

9 781782 224914